Beyond Redundancy

More than ever before, people, in pursuing their career paths, are likely to face the shock of redundancy. This book gives sound practical and psychological advice on how to cope and shows the way forward 'beyond redundancy'.

GW00703459

Beyond Redundancy

by

Christopher Bainton
& Theresa Crowley

Thorsons
An Imprint of HarperCollins*Publishers*

Thorsons
An Imprint of HarperCollins*Publishers*
77–85 Fulham Palace Road,
Hammersmith, London W6 8JB

First published as *Redundancy* by Turnstone Press in 1985
This fully revised edition published by Thorsons 1992
1 3 5 7 9 10 8 6 4 2

A catalogue record for this book
is available from the British Library

ISBN 0 7225 7222 1

Typeset by Harper Phototypesetters Limited,
Northampton, England
Printed in Great Britain by
Hartnolls Ltd, Bodmin, Cornwall

Contents

Introduction

Redundancy, once the exception, is now if not exactly the rule more likely than not to interrupt the majority of people's careers at least once. Whereas it was principally regarded – especially in the late seventies and early eighties – as a device to shake out overmanning in manufacturing industries, by cutting away unskilled and semi-skilled workforces who had become superfluous through developments in technology, the late eighties and early nineties presented a very different picture. The focus swung away from shop-floor workers in what remained of the smoke-stack industries in the Midlands and North, and widened to include hitherto impregnable territory – London and the South-East.

White-collar jobs have been the hardest hit sector in this region and, although no one industry has remained immune from the effects of redundancy, the worst affected areas have been those that appeared most vulnerable during the eighties' boom. Banking and financial institutions in the City, estate agency chains, the computer industry, construction and the service and retail sectors have all had to decimate staff. Even those businesses such as the major accountancy firms which had built profitable practices advising client companies on how to restructure, rationalize and divest – euphemisms for laying people off – had to bite the bullet and make substantial numbers of their own staff redundant. No one person could be regarded as safe, whether they were clerical assistants or board directors in any commercial or industrial sector.

The causes for this are complicated and diverse and range from geo-political considerations, through political machinations and demographic changes to the continuing development of technology. It is not the purpose of this book to analyse these nor to decide what went wrong: it is simply to offer a practical guide to those who have been made redundant, those who are about to be and those who although currently not under threat, are looking to make a positive move to a better career opportunity. In these respects, the book is unashamedly a job hunter's guide. We also look at some of the practical difficulties – especially the financial ones – facing the newly redundant person and offer advice on how to deal with them, and examine alternatives to conventional employment: using redundancy as a launch pad into a different lifestyle.

Above all, we look at the psychological effects of redundancy and how these can be managed to your best advantage. To draw a parallel: one of the main reasons why the recession in the early nineties lasted longer and was more severe than anticipated was generally attributed to a lack of confidence in recovery. One can apply the same argument to a particular individual – lack of confidence in one's ability to secure a new job will almost certainly hinder one's attempts. The longer this process continues, the more difficult it is to maintain one's confidence and belief in oneself, which further delays recovery in the sense of landing that job.

If, at this moment, you are without a job because of redundancy, the chances are that you will either think of yourself or hear others describe you as a redundant person. There is no such thing. Jobs are made redundant and not people. Although in cold print this may look trite, or even clichéd, it is an important fact to remember in terms of maintaining your self-esteem and thus your confidence. The job you used to do ceased to exist. So now you have to find another.

If you have been made redundant, it is important to take charge of the situation. It is very easy to feel that you are a pawn in some management game and a victim of circumstances that are totally beyond your control. Do not be a passive recipient, waiting to find out what will be doled out to you. Instead, for your own well-being and morale, you need to feel that you are in control of the situation and not that events control you.

Psychologists talk about 'locus of control'. Those who have an external locus of control feel that events control them – that luck or fate will decide what happens to them. Those with an internal locus of control feel that they are in control of events. They make their own destiny and will overcome difficulties through their own determination and talent. An internal locus of control is essential for anyone who has been made redundant. When people first get over the shock of redundancy, they will often have this automatically. In the first stages of unemployment, most people will be busy job-hunting – writing applications, visiting agencies, buying newspapers, attending interviews and actively helping themselves. If an optimistic frame of mind is to be sustained, this active approach must also be maintained.

How can you achieve this? Firstly, you should not meekly accept whatever help your employer offers, but work out for yourself what your needs are; secondly, ask your employer to help you meet those needs. The type of help employers can provide, details of which we give in the following chapter, gives some prompters as to what your needs might be. The two major needs are likely to be adequate finances to see you through any period of unemployment, and help in finding another job. We explore these more fully in Chapters 2 and 3.

Remaining positive and confident has been highlighted as the key to coping with your new situation. It is particularly difficult to maintain this attitude when you talk to other people about your redundancy. There are two levels to this: one is talking about it with your partner and family; the other with your friends, colleagues and business contacts. Contacting this latter group now falls under the rather trendy categorization of 'networking'. We talk about the value of this later in terms of getting business contacts to help you find a job.

But why worry your family – especially if you are at the stage where redundancy is likely, but the axe has yet to fall? Giving them some prior warning has considerable advantages. The threat of redundancy is likely to make you tense, which in turn can put a strain on relationships. It is far better to be open about it, so you can all pull together. This works both on a practical level, in terms of reducing your less essential expenditure, for example, and also as a source of morale-boosting support.

While on the hunt for a job you are likely to experience mood swings. Over and above the daily fluctuations, there will be a certain change in attitude over time. Research on redundancy and unemployment from the 1930s on has shown a common pattern of reaction to job loss:

1. *Shock* – You cannot accept or believe what has happened and cannot believe it has happened to you.
2. *Optimism* – You feel that 'something will turn up'; a new job will be found quickly and, in the meantime, there is a lump sum of redundancy money to act as a cushion.
3. *Pessimism* – 'Something' has not turned up, and the redundancy capital has been eroded by a dream holiday or the monthly reality of the mortgage payments.
4. *Fatalism* – Unemployment is accepted and you settle into a routine of getting up late and doing very little.

How to get over phase 1 and how to remain in phase 2 until you secure a new career start is discussed in Chapter 5.

Coping with the shock of redundancy and getting the best deal in terms of compensation benefits, employer and government help, while being fully engaged in job hunting, is a complex and time-consuming process. This book is designed as a step-by-step guide to take you beyond redundancy and into a more positive future.

Chapter 1
Opening Moves

What is Redundancy?

Whether wrapped in extended notice periods and golden handshakes, or dismissal at half an hour's notice, redundancy means enforced job loss. Redundancy is currently affecting hundreds of thousands of workers a year. The scale of the problem is enormous.

If the overall redundancy figures are high, some types of employees are undoubtedly affected more than others. Although much publicity is given to the difficulties faced by the older redundant workers, the unemployment rate declines with age up until 54. After 54 it is still much lower than it is for 20 to 24 year olds. What is apparent from the figures however is that all age groups are affected by redundancy. The same is true for all occupation groups.

When the term 'unemployment' first appeared in the *Encyclopaedia Britannica* in 1911, it was described as 'a condition of being unemployed amongst the working classes'. This is no longer the case. Unemployment has increasingly affected those at the top as well as those at the bottom of the occupational tree. Unemployment has steadily increased amongst managerial and professional workers. The unskilled however continue to form a major proportion of the unemployed and redundant, despite the increased vulnerability of white collar workers. The white collar worker remains at a considerable advantage when it comes to finding new employment. The proportion of jobs available to the unskilled has steadily declined even as their unemployed numbers have increased and this trend is likely to continue for the foreseeable future. The decline in jobs for the unskilled has been matched by a steady increase in jobs for the skilled and well-qualified, a trend which is also likely to continue. Those at risk will continue to be those who lack skills and qualifications and those with little work experience, whom employers will have least qualms about losing when redundancies must be made.

Although redundancy has become more common at all levels it is still thought by many of those affected by it as a stigma. This is especially true of white collar or managerial staff who, prior to the current recession, were unlikely to be greatly affected. Redundancy is not something to be ashamed of, and perhaps more importantly, is not seen by and large to be a stigma or something to be ashamed of by potential employers. In an employer survey, carried out by the Unemployment Research Unit, many employers were anxious to reassure the unemployed on that point:

> *I don't think there is a stigma. Certainly there was in the past. If you saw a person unemployed, you'd think, 'Hello, what's he been up to? Something's gone wrong somewhere.' Today I don't think there's a stigma at all. It's like an illness. You've just got caught up in the disease.*
>
> Director, machine tool company

> *I think society's attitude is changing. In a society where full employment was the norm, people tended to look upon someone unemployed as a layabout and a scrounger living on Social Security etc. These were rather extreme views, but it represented an attitude of mind because people had been accustomed to the fact that everybody had a job. Then the recession came and those attitudes still came through, but eventually people who were holding those attitudes, suddenly, bang, they found themselves unemployed.*
>
> Personnel Manager, electronics company.

The redundant are no longer the social lepers of yesteryear. Redundancy is something which can, and increasingly will, happen to large numbers of people – not just once, but several times in their working lives. Unemployment and redundancy are likely to become increasingly common not only when the economy takes a downturn, but also as the accelerating rate of industrial innovation and change brings about changes in job definitions and company structures to meet the demands of new technology and new products.

The Mechanics of Redundancy

Under the Employment Protection (Consolidation) Act 1978, employment which is terminated is defined as redundancy if a work place is closing down, or because fewer employees of a particular kind are (or are expected to be) needed. Normally, the employee's job must have disappeared. It is not redundancy if that employer immediately engages a direct replacement, though it does not affect the issue if the employer is recruiting more workers of a different type, or in some other location (*unless* the dismissed employees were requested under their contracts to move to the new location). However, where employees are dismissed because of a need to reduce the overall workforce and the remaining workforce move into different jobs, someone may be moved into the job left vacant by a departing employee. Provided the replacements leave vacancies elsewhere in the organization and there is a net loss of jobs, those dismissed qualify for redundancy payments.

The legislation in the UK lays down the length of notice which employees are entitled to receive of their redundancy and the monetary compensation the redundant employee is entitled to receive. There are however a number of groups of employees who are not protected by the legislation such as Crown Servants, the police and armed forces, civil servants, Health Service employees, dockyard workers and merchant seamen, all of whose conditions of work make alternative arrangements for terminating their employment should the need arise. The legislation also makes no provision for those with less than two years service (service before the age of 18 does not count); part-time employees who work less than 8 hours per week, part-time employees with less than five years' service who work between 8 and

16 hours per week, those on fixed-term contracts which include (with their written agreement) a clause waiving entitlement to a redundancy payment, those who normally work overseas, and those over retirement age or under 20. Days lost through industrial disputes do not count towards length of service.

Employees who are fully covered are entitled to receive financial compensation, time off from work to attend job interviews and a specified notice period. Even groups who are not entitled to receive financial compensation because of length of service or other factors, will usually be entitled to the other benefits. The employer is also required by law to give notice to the Department of Employment that redundancies are to be made if ten or more employees are involved. When the company is unionized, employers are obliged to consult with the trade unions and inform them of the reasons for the redundancies, the numbers and descriptions of employees they are making redundant, the total numbers of employees of that type employed at the location concerned, the proposed method of selecting employees for redundancy and the method of carrying out the redundancies.

Once the individuals concerned have been selected, they must be given notice of their redundancy. The length of notice required will depend upon their length of service and amounts to one week's notice for each year's service up to a maximum of twelve years.

Those who qualify for redundancy payments receive half a week's pay for each year of employment between the ages of 18 and 21; one week's pay for each year of employment between the ages of 22 and 40; and one and a half week's pay for each year of employment over the age of 40 but below the age of 65, up to a maximum of twenty years. When an employee is within 12 months of statutory retirement age, the redundancy entitlement is reduced by one twelfth for each complete month thus reducing it to nothing by retirement age. In addition there is an upper wage limit which is regularly reviewed. This was £184 per week from 1 April 1990. The number of weeks' redundancy pay can be calculated by the ready reckoner at the back of this book. The entitlement of those earning more will be based on the maximum wage. Where wages vary because of bonus, commission etc., the wages of the previous twelve weeks are taken to produce an average rate of pay. Once you have been given notice of redundancy, you can then take time off for job hunting providing prior warning is given. You are entitled to time off for interviews and also for visiting jobcentres, agencies etc.

The terms above are the statutory ones laid down by the legislation. They represent the *minimum* notice periods, financial compensation and job-hunting help which employers can offer. Many employers will either want to offer, or have been persuaded by trade unions and their employees that they should offer more generous terms than these. In larger companies, particularly, there are likely to be written redundancy agreements negotiated with the unions which will give increased financial compensation. The terms on which individuals become redundant can therefore vary. Additional benefits which the employer may offer redundant employees are discussed later, but the result is the same – job loss.

Redeployment

In some cases, you will not automatically be offered redundancy, but may be offered redeployment in either another job at your present location or another job at an alternative location. Your company may offer you redeployment but allow you to take the option of redundancy as an alternative. In this situation you will need to weigh up the job offer as you would any other job offer which came from outside. Is the job you have been offered a job you would enjoy doing? What are the prospects? If a move is involved, is it to a part of the country where you would like to live? What are the prospects for alternative jobs? Could you find yourself an equally good job in another company and still collect your redundancy money from your present firm? If you are offered optional redeployment you will usually be given some time to think it over. If you are uncertain what to do, it is a good idea to explore the job prospects in other companies.

If you think your chances of gaining employment elsewhere are good, the redundancy package may be more attractive than an alternative job. But before making a decision do some research. Do not blithely think, 'Of course I'll be able to get another job!' Even if you have had no trouble in finding jobs before, you may find the economic and job climate somewhat different from the last time you were on the market. Scan the job ads carefully and see how many there are which would be suitable for you. Approach the private and public job agencies and get some idea of the job availability for your particular expertise. Consider also the pensions aspect and how much you would lose by leaving your present scheme.

The offer of redeployment may not be optional. If your employer offers you 'suitable' alternative employment and you refuse this unreasonably, you will not be able to claim a redundancy payment. The difficulty here is in defining suitability. The factors taken into consideration are travel time, remuneration, status, job duties and general practice regarding mobility in the industry concerned.

Under the terms of the Employment Protection (Consolidation) Act 1978 the employer must adhere to the following procedure when offering redeployment. Before the employee's current contract of employment comes to an end, the employer offers to renew the contract of employment or to re-engage the employee in an alternative capacity. The offer should preferably be in writing with a job description to enable the employee to decide whether the alternative is suitable or not. This offer of renewal should take effect either immediately on the ending of the previous contract or after an interval of not more than four weeks from that time. Either the provision of the new or renewed contract relating to the capacity and place in which the employee will be employed and as to other terms and conditions of employment will not differ from the corresponding provisions of the previous contract; or the capacity, place or other terms will differ wholly or in part, but the offer still represents an offer of suitable employment. The offer must relate to the same employer or an associated or successor employer who has taken over the business.

There is a four-week statutory trial period during which the employee can try an alternative job. This period can also be extended to allow for any training necessary for the new job. Once the trial period has expired, the new job will normally be deemed to have been accepted, but if before the expiry of the trial period the employee decides he does not wish to take the new job, he can leave and claim redundancy compensation for the loss of his old job. If however the employer argues that the new job was 'suitable' and refuses to pay, the employee will be obliged to take the matter to an Industrial Tribunal.

If a new job is offered to you, you should establish with your employer whether or not the company regards this as a 'suitable' job and whether they will be willing to give you redundancy compensation if you refuse it. If you will be given redundancy as an alternative, then you have nothing to lose in trying out the new job. If however you think that you and your employer are likely to disagree about the suitability of an alternative job, you will have to do some thinking.

The problem with taking your employer to an Industrial Tribunal is that you may find it difficult to get another employer to take you on afterwards. Although this is very unjust, employers look warily upon employees who have been involved in Industrial Tribunals. You will need to weigh up the amount of redundancy compensation you are likely to lose by not fighting your case and how much longer you are likely to be working. If you are nearing retirement age, your redundancy payment is likely to be larger and more important to you than for someone younger with only a few years service in their company. If you are near retiring age you may not be able to get employment again anyway and there are fewer disadvantages in taking a case to a Tribunal and more financially to gain. A younger person will have more to lose by being branded a trouble-maker and may be better advised to take the alternative job as an interim measure and then devote time looking for something better elsewhere. Another alternative if you do decide to press a claim is to try and get yourself a new job before you start pursuing the claim, so that you are safely settled with another employer before the proceedings start.

Whatever decision you make, it is not one to be made in the heat of the moment. Before taking any action you should seek the advice of a trade union official, solicitor or Citizens Advice Bureau. It is easy to threaten to sue your employer because you are upset and angry over a proposed redeployment, but to safeguard your own interests, you should make sure that you have a case before getting involved. What appears to you to be a watertight and reasonable case may, because of some technicality, not be so in the eyes of the law.

Application forms and information on how to claim and the time limits for claims can be obtained from jobcentres or Unemployment Benefit Offices. The claim can be lodged as soon as notice has been given but must reach the Central Office of Industrial Tribunals before the expiry of the time limit.

Unfair Selection for Redundancy

The Employment Protection (Consolidation) Act also lays down grounds under which it is unreasonable to dismiss a particular employee. Employers have to justify not only that it was reasonable to dismiss *an* employee, but also that it was reasonable to dismiss *that* employee. The main grounds whereby redundancy may be considered unfair are where people are selected because of trade union activities or where they are selected in contravention of an established practice, such as last-in-first-out. Cases have also been successful where a form of redundancy selection was held to be indirectly discriminatory against women or ethnic minorities. As with offers of alternative employment, you will need to take legal advice before pressing any claim against your employer.

Short-time Working and Lay-offs

An employee who has been laid off and paid no wages, or kept on short time and received less than half a week's pay for four or more consecutive weeks or for six or more weeks within a thirteen-week period can qualify for redundancy. In order to claim, the employee must give written notice of his intention within four weeks of the lay-off or short-time finishing. Again the legislation is complicated and you should take appropriate advice about the correct procedure if you are thinking of claiming redundancy.

Problems in Obtaining Redundancy Compensation

When a company is unable to pay its redundancy payments because of insolvency, the Department of Employment will make payments direct to the employees concerned. The employer will be given application forms to distribute to his employees for completion. In addition employees can claim for arrears of pay and money in lieu of notice etc. if these have not been paid. If your employer does not follow this procedure, you should contact the Department of Employment's local office for advice. Before reimbursing an employee, the Department of Employment must be satisfied that the employer is insolvent and must have received a statement from the receiver, liquidator or trustee that the employee is entitled to the debt claimed. This latter requirement can however be waived if there is likely to be an unreasonable delay.

When an employer has not paid the statutory redundancy compensation for some other reason, the employee must show that he intends making a claim within six months of the 'relevant date' of dismissal. The 'relevant date' is taken to be the date when notice expires if the contract is terminated by notice, or the date when termination takes effect if money is paid in lieu of notice. The employee can show his intention of claiming by giving written notice to his employer that he wants payment. This can be a simple dated claim in writing along the lines of: 'I claim that I was dismissed by reason of redundancy and that I am entitled to a redundancy payment.' A copy should be kept by the employee. If the employer refuses to pay, the matter will have to be taken to an Industrial Tribunal. Alternatively, an employee can immediately refer the question as to his right to payment or the amount of payment to a tribunal, or can present a complaint of unfair dismissal to a tribunal. If a tribunal awards a redundancy payment and the employer still does not pay, the employee should seek the advice of the local Redundancy Payments Office.

Pension Rights

There are usually a number of options available as far as pension rights are concerned. These are: to obtain a refund of your contributions; to leave your pension where it is; to transfer your pension into a new employer's scheme; or to take early retirement and an immediate pension. The merits of each will depend on your age and the relative benefits of your old scheme compared with any new scheme. If you are within a few years of retiring age your employer may be willing to offer you an early retirement pension. If you think you will have difficulty in securing a new job, this may be a good option. Often employers will offer enhanced immediate pensions for older redundant employees and this could be a good option, particularly if the scheme allows you to exchange part of your pension for a lump sum cash payment. If you have been paying into your pension scheme for less than five years, you can usually if you wish take a cash refund. The refund will be subject to tax at 10 per cent. Advice as to the best course in your particular case can be obtained from your company's pension manager, or if you feel you need outside advice you can go to an independent pensions consultant. Alternatively your trade union may be able to help you.

Severance Packages

Under the heading 'The Mechanics of Redundancy', earlier in this chapter, a description was given of the minimum benefits which the employee could expect from the employer. In many instances, however the employer will be willing to offer more. Where the company has negotiated a written redundancy agreement, financial compensation will have been thrashed out, but where there is no written provision this is an area where pressure can be brought on the employer to provide more than the basic requirements. If a number of people are to be made redundant, then they will obviously need to negotiate together, either through a union representative if they have one, or through a spokesperson elected from amongst themselves. This is an area where careful research is likely to stand those involved in good stead. Most employers are reasonable people and have considerable goodwill towards their redundant staff. Research amongst similar companies will show what is the 'going rate' for redundancy packages in your area and industry. Likely sources of information are union officials in other companies, advisers at unemployed people's self-help groups, and the local and industry press.

What employers are prepared to offer will obviously be limited by the company's financial situation. Where the redundancies are very extensive or a complete site closure is involved, then money will be tight and the employer will be subject to financial constraints. In this situation, the employer may not be able or willing to offer employees more cash, but may be able to help in other ways. Where the redundancies are fewer, there will be fewer limitations to the financial compensation which can be provided and if no offer of compensation above the statutory minimum has been made, this point will be worth pursuing.

What benefits are employers willing to provide and what should the employee ask for? The Unemployment Research Unit found that the majority of companies were willing to provide additional benefits to those laid down by law. Below is a list of some of the benefits they mentioned.

- Approaching other employers about jobs for their redundant employees
- Job-hunting advice – where to look for jobs, how to write applications, how to prepare CVs, and how to behave at interviews
- Additional financial compensation
- Giving advice on state benefits, investment of redundancy money, financial planning for unemployment
- Psychological counselling on dealing with job loss
- Paying for the services of careers counsellors or outplacement consultants
- Relocation expenses for people who have found jobs in new areas
- Long notice-periods
- Keeping people nominally employed while job hunting

The majority of employers were willing to provide some combination if not all of the above benefits. The majority of employers therefore are willing to help. Some however may not understand what kinds of help and advice are needed by employees, and may not have thought of providing certain kinds of help – particularly if they have not had to handle redundancies before. The trend is in fact for employers to become increasingly involved in the welfare of their redundant staff. The way has been led by the larger companies, many of whom have been faced in recent years with situations where they have had to close down factories or offices that were the main employers in areas with little alternative employment. Increasingly employers have become involved in providing alternative work for those whom they make redundant. One of the leading companies in the field has been British Steel (Industry) Ltd, a subsidiary of British Steel. This company's sole purpose was to create new jobs in areas where British Steel withdrew its commitment, by attracting new industry.

Personal Reaction

These are all areas of positive help which can be provided for the person being made redundant. The difficulty is in feeling sufficiently composed and assertive to ask for help. The inclination is to disinvolve oneself from the past employer as quickly as possible. Many people who have been made redundant feel not only shocked but also irrationally guilty. Unless the terms on which people have been selected for redundancy are very clear, the inevitable question arises, 'Why me? What have I done wrong? Why did they pick on me?' Such self-doubt is not helpful when dealing with one's employer. Why you were made redundant is not particularly important at this stage, but what is important is how to cope with the situation. Work out what your needs might be and if you have any friends who have been made redundant, seek their advice on this. If your employer has not offered the kind of help you think you might need, do not be afraid to ask. The fact that you have not been offered certain help does not mean that your employer is unwilling to provide it. He or she may be only too willing to help you. The majority of employers have not as yet experienced redundancy themselves and may not realize what they could do to help. Unless someone has the initiative to make suggestions, it may not occur to employers that there is a lot they can do to set you on the right road to re-employment.

Employers should be aware that the employee may be in no position to take any sensible stock of his or her situation. The employer can be in a better position to appraise employees' needs than they will be themselves at a time when they will not be at their most objective. By softening the blow of redundancy with offers of positive help and advice, employers not only prevent the employee sinking into shell-shocked inertia but help them to take active steps to deal with the situation, they also make the situation a lot easier for themselves. Morale will be much higher amongst those staff not affected by the redundancies if the employer can be seen to be working to help those employees affected. Often employers shirk discussing with their redundant staff the difficulties of job hunting and the financial problems they may face whilst looking for another job. It is embarrassing and unpleasant to have to deal with redundancies, but for the employee's sake the difficulties must not be glossed over; they must be discussed objectively and realistically and then tackled with positive suggestions on how to overcome them.

If your employer whom you have always trusted to 'do right' by you has let you down by handling the redundancy badly, how are you to react? One of the best ways of dealing with your feelings is to put yourself in your boss's place. How would you have felt if you had had to tell a valued and long-standing employee that you could no longer keep him or her? Easy though it is to say, 'I would never have treated any employee of mine like this,' how many of us are successful in telling others unpalatable truths? How many of us will sidestep the issue and try to avoid directly telling the person? The answer is quite a few. If you have been badly treated, don't develop a grudge against your employer. He or she is probably well aware that things have been handled badly and will not need reminding of it by you. Many employers describe having to tell people that they are redundant as the worst thing that can happen to them in their job:

It's terrible. It's terrible even dismissing somebody to the extent that they've loused up their job, but to say that a guy's lost his job and really he's done a good job, but because of this factor or that factor he's now unemployed, yes, it's terrible. Show me a guy who doesn't think about dismissing people for whatever reason, doesn't care about it, that's got to be a bad manager.

Personnel Director: construction company

If your employer has not handled the situation in the most tactful way, he will probably feel guilty about it and this can be an advantage when it comes to negotiating the severance package.

You now know what redundancy is, and have some idea of the help your employer is likely to offer you to support you financially in any period of unemployment and to help you regain employment. We will now turn to that most pressing of practical problems – money.

Chapter 2

Financing Redundancy

Despite the publicity given to the 'golden handshakes' paid to company chairmen etc., most people do not walk away with enormous sums of money when their jobs disappear. Many people have not worked for their employers for long enough to be entitled to any money at all.

As we mentioned earlier, if you are dissatisfied with the financial provision your employer offers, do not just accept the situation. Present a reasoned case for being offered more. If your company has folded and there is no money in the kitty, you will not be able to get any additional assistance, but many redundancies do not involve complete company shut-downs. You are more likely to be the victim of staff cutbacks and rationalization than complete bankruptcy. Companies are always keen to maintain good community relations, and a word to the editor of the local newspaper that Bloggs Brothers are making people redundant and that staff are in the process of negotiating redundancy terms, will alert your employer to the fact that people are taking note of what is going on.

When your redundancy payment has been settled and you leave the company, your employer must give you a written statement indicating how the statutory part of your redundancy pay has been calculated. You will also receive any additional redundancy money your employer is prepared to pay, plus your last pay cheque, any money in lieu of holiday entitlement and money in lieu of notice if your company has not asked you to work your notice period.

Redundancy payments below a certain limit, currently £30,000, are not taxable, so unless you are in the real 'golden handshake' league, you will not need tax advice. If you are in this bracket, you should seek advice from tax planning experts on how to minimize your contribution to the state.

Many people who become redundant receive a large sum of money for the first time in their lives. The question is what to do with it, and what not to do with it. Particularly, if your redundancy payment brings your savings over the £8,000 limit where you cannot claim Income Support, you will probably need to use some of the money to live on. You will need expert advice on how to invest your money to supplement your income. Your employer may be willing to help with investment advice or to recommend sources of help. Sometimes, companies are unwilling to provide financial advice themselves because they have visions of being sued should anything go wrong, but they may be willing to suggest the name of a third party such as a bank. You can also contact your own bank and/or building society manager. Weigh up their advice carefully. Banks and building societies are obviously eager to sell their own products and you will have to decide which is offering the best package for you.

Whatever you do, remember that you may have to make this money last some time, so however tempting it is to make a special purchase which you have always wanted – don't. You may find yourself sitting gloomily looking at a pile of bills long after the tan of that special holiday has faded.

Claiming Benefit

Once you have ceased to be employed, you should make arrangements to claim state benefits. This applies whether you have been selected for redundancy or have volunteered. There are two main types of benefit that you may be able to claim: Unemployment Benefit, which is administered by the Department of Employment, and Income Support administered by the Department of Social Security. Unemployment Benefit is based on your National Insurance contributions and is not means-tested. Income Support requires no National Insurance contributions and is means-tested. Unemployment Benefit can be claimed for up to a year, after which you will have to rely on means-tested benefits.

If you have worked out your notice period, you may be entitled to sign on for Unemployment Benefit on the working day after your employment finished. If you have not worked your notice, but have been paid money in lieu of notice, you will not be entitled to receive benefit until the period covered by the money in lieu of notice has expired. In addition, the Social Security Act 1989 specifies that any additional money which your employer pays, to you above your statutory redundancy payment can be treated as though it is salary in lieu of notice. At the end of this period, however, you will still be eligible for Unemployment Benefit for up to one year. In any event, although you should sign on immediately after your employment finishes, you will not be entitled to any money for the first three days of your claim. However, it is important to register as soon as you can, so that you do not have any gaps in your National Insurance contribution record.

To make a claim for Unemployment Benefit, you must contact the Employment Service which is the executive agency of the Department of Employment that controls Unemployment Benefit Offices and jobcentres. The Employment Service is in the process of amalgamating its Unemployment Benefit Offices, which pay out benefit, and its jobcentres which help find you a job. In some areas you will visit a separate Unemployment Benefit Office to claim unemployment benefit, and in other areas there will be a 'one-stop' integrated Employment Centre covering benefits and jobs. You will be able to find your own local office by looking in the telephone book under 'Employment Service'.

Once you have located the office for your area, you need to make an appointment to see a New Client Adviser. You can make the appointment by telephoning or calling in. The opening hours of Benefit Offices vary, but 9 a.m. to 3.30 p.m., Monday to Thursday, and 10 a.m. to 3.30 p.m. on Fridays, are typical.

Before seeing the New Client Adviser, you will need to complete the claims forms. You can either collect these when you visit the office to make your appointment or immediately before your appointment with the New Client

Adviser. One of the forms you will be given is a UB671. The questions cover the type of work you have been doing, your qualifications and experience, the type of work you are seeking, the hours and salary you are prepared to accept, your health and how you intend to look for work. The aim is to establish that you are available for and actively seeking employment. You will also be given form UB461 – the Claim for Unemployment Benefit – which you sign at the interview with the New Client Adviser.

When you see the New Client Adviser, you will need your P45 or other evidence of your National Insurance number. The New Client adviser will go through the UB671 with you. You will then be given a 'Back to Work Plan' which contains a job goal or goals and suggested methods of searching for a job. You may also be offered the option of taking up certain types of training. These are discussed later in the book. You will also be given a booklet called *Helping you back to work – Information for Claimants*. This spells out your responsibility as a claimant to be 'actively seeking employment', and gives you information on benefits and how to 'sign on'.

The last stage of the interview with the New Claimant Adviser will be to take your claim for benefit. If you have dependent children, you should also ask for and complete form UB534.

Unless your savings take you well above the £8,000 limit, you should also claim Income Support as well as claiming Unemployment Benefit and ask for form B1. You should complete this and send or take it to your local office of the Department of Social Security. The Employment Service staff may or may not volunteer the information about claiming Income Support, but there are a number of reasons why it is a good idea to do so.

Firstly, you may find that there is a delay before you start to receive Unemployment Benefit and you may be entitled to receive Income Support while you are waiting for your Unemployment Benefit claim to be processed. Unemployment Benefit is difficult to calculate and it may take some time to 'get you on the computer'. You cannot receive benefit until your employer has received and returned a form to the Employment Service which confirms that you have not left your employment voluntarily (volunteering for redundancy does not count as voluntary leaving) and that you have not been dismissed for misconduct.

Secondly, Income Support is calculated not by how much you have contributed to the system but by your 'needs'. If your 'needs' exceed your Unemployment Benefit, it can be topped up by Income Support.

Thirdly, you may have the unpleasant surprise of discovering that you are not entitled to Unemployment Benefit. Your entitlement depends on whether you paid sufficient National Insurance contributions in the tax year ending before the January of the year in which you claim. This rather complicated formula means that if you were claiming benefit in November 1992, to qualify you would have to have paid sufficient contributions in the tax year ending 5 April 1991.

Fourthly, if you receive Income Support, you are also entitled to other useful free benefits such as free prescriptions, free school meals, free dental care, free spectacles and milk and vitamin tokens if you have children under school age.

The system is so complicated that no one will be able to tell you immediately if you are eligible for Unemployment Benefit. You will have to wait until your claim has been processed and you receive either a notice explaining that your contributions were for some reason deficient, or you receive your first girocheque for Unemployment Benefit. If you are not eligible for Unemployment Benefit and have not claimed Income Support, you will not be able to back-date your claim for Income Support. Because of these uncertainties, it is much better to claim Income Support while you wait for your unemployment claim to be processed. If your claim for either Unemployment Benefit or Income Support is refused and you disagree with the decision you can appeal. The note which informs you that you have been refused benefit will also explain the appeals procedure. If you do run into problems, you should also seek the advice of your local claimants union or welfare rights organization. A list of these is given at the back of the book.

If you have over £8,000 in savings you will not be able to claim Income Support. If your savings are between £3,000 and £8,000, your Income Support will be reduced by £1 for every £250 of savings between £3,000 and £8,000. This is to ensure that people do not claim Income Support who do not really need it. You are not allowed to give away or simply dispose of your savings in order to qualify for Income Support. Transferring a lump sum to another person, transferring the title of a property which is not your main home to another person or putting your savings in trust for yourself or another person would all disqualify you from receiving Income Support. You can spend your savings 'reasonably' on day-to-day living expenses, home improvements, a holiday, furniture or a non-expensive car, but you should keep notes on how you have spent your money and receipts for any large outgoings.

Once your Unemployment Benefit and/or Income Support claim has been processed and you are 'on the computer', you should receive a fortnightly girocheque in the post, unless you live at an address which has been 'black-listed' for some reason. In this case, you will have to collect your girocheque from the benefit office. The girocheque will cover both your Unemployment Benefit and Income Support. Once you have started signing on, it is important that you attend punctually. If you do not do the right things at the right time, you may find yourself in a game of administrative snakes and ladders and have to start all over again from the beginning!

All these administrative complexities may sound very daunting and at times you may wonder if the whole process is designed to discourage people from claiming at all. Everything may happen very smoothly, but the system can at times be slow and frustrating. A good policy when attending the offices for interviews is to take something to read and a sandwich. At least this way, you can pass the time if you do end up waiting.

Some of the offices are newly furbished and very smart, others much less so. If your local office retains the screwed-to-the-floor chairs and smash-proof glass screens, it is not the best way to start off your career as a job-seeker, but try not to be disheartened. Similarly, staff will vary in their attitude. Usually they are very helpful, but they are often working under considerable pressure, so don't be put off if the 'customer care' you receive is not all it should be. The focus of the New Client Adviser interview is getting you back into work as soon as possible, rather than helping you with your benefit claim, so make sure that matters such as the BI form for Income Support are not forgotten.

The British are not noted for their ability to be forthcoming about themselves. Answering a lot of personal questions, sometimes to someone much younger than yourself, can be embarrassing at first, but again – don't be put off. The staff are not trying to be deliberately intrusive but are simply following instructions.

If it all seems too horribly confusing, ask some of the other claimants at the office what to do. 'Old hands' are usually delighted to steer you through the maze.

Budgeting for Unemployment

The rates for Unemployment Benefit and Income Support are upgraded each year in the budget and increases take effect in November. The rates should be publicized in benefit and social security offices. Unless you have been used to a very low income, the rates may come as a bit of a shock. You will have to do some careful budgeting.

Many people find a job before leaving their former firm or within a few weeks of leaving, but many people can remain unemployed for a year or more. You will need to take account of this when budgeting. A typical list might contain the following items:

Mortgage repayments/Rent
Community Charge/Council Tax
Electricity
Gas
Telephone
Water
Loans and HP
Food/Household items
Cigarettes/Drink
Car – tax, MOT, insurance and petrol
Clothing and dry cleaning
Entertainment and holidays
Subscriptions to professional bodies, clubs etc.
Children's school and leisure expenses
Miscellaneous

Having calculated your expenditure, you now need to calculate your income. If you have received redundancy compensation you will have to decide how best to make your money work for you. If you have well over the amount where you are allowed to claim Income Support, you will need to use your capital to supplement your income. Your income will therefore consist of your Unemployment Benefit, plus interest from redundancy payments and other savings and/or Income Support. The Unemployment Benefit which you receive for yourself and an adult dependant is now taxable, but Income Support is not taxable. This does not mean that your benefit is taxed fortnightly as you receive it. It means that when your tax liability for the year is calculated, your benefits will be treated as income. The amount of tax you paid while you were working may have covered your tax liability and you may be entitled to a tax rebate, but you will not receive this until the end of the tax year or until you find a new job, whichever is sooner. If at the end of the tax year you have paid insufficient benefit, your coding will be adjusted to recoup the deficit when you go back to work.

Having got advice on how to invest your redundancy money and established what your income is likely to be, you can now begin to tailor your expenditure to your income. Examine each item on your expenditure list and think about how you can reduce your expenditure to the minimum.

Housing

With the current controversy over the rising rate of repossessions by building societies, most people will be aware of the difficulties and dangers of falling behind with mortgage repayments. One of the largest items on your budget is likely to be housing. In addition, to your Unemployment Benefit or Income Support, you may be able to get Housing Benefit to help you with your housing costs.

If you claim Income Support, a claim form for Housing Benefit will be included with form B1. This will be sent on from the Department of Social Security to your Local Authority when you make your Income Support claim. If you are an owner-occupier, you may get help with any interest you pay on a loan or mortgage you have taken out to purchase your home. If you and your partner are aged under 60, you will receive 50 per cent of your mortgage interest for the first 16 weeks of your Income Support claim. Thereafter, you will receive the full amount of interest. If you are renting your home, you may receive help with your rent. Depending on your income, you may also receive help with rent if you do not receive Income Support. You should apply for this direct to your local authority.

If you receive Income Support, you will only have to pay 20 per cent of the Community Charge and if you receive Unemployment Benefit, you may be eligible for a reduction because of your drop in earnings. All this will change to some extent with the introduction of the new Council Tax, but similar assistance is likely to be available.

Any help you receive with your mortgage will cover only the interest repayments, not the capital repayment.

If your capital repayment is small, it is best to try and make up the difference if you can. If this is beyond your means, you will have to ask your building society or bank to 'reschedule' your mortgage. This means that the lender agrees to accept interest-only payments for a period. This has become common practice since redundancy has become more widespread and there should be no problem in rescheduling for some months. If your unemployment is prolonged, however, you may have to think about selling your property and moving to a cheaper one. The majority of unemployed people do manage to maintain their mortgage repayments and problems arise mainly when people fail to tell their bank or building society of their problem and simply do not pay. Even if you think you can manage to continue the full amount, it is wise to tell your building society or bank manager about your situation so that he or she is forewarned should there be problems later on. New ways of taking the burden on mortgage payers are currently being introduced by banks and building societies (under pressure from the government), and it is wise to discuss your situation with them individually before it becomes an issue or problem.

Utilities

Payments for utilities comprise another large chunk of most people's outgoings. The various utilities are sympathetic and will allow some delay in payment if you are made redundant, but the money will have to be paid sooner or later and it is unwise to get into debt with them. Some utilities operate budget payment systems whereby you pay a fixed amount each month which is assessed from your previous annual consumption. This has the advantage of preventing the arrival of sudden horrific bills at a time when you are going to find it difficult to produce large sums of money. Banks also provide a budget account service, whereby they calculate the amount needed for all such outgoings, allowing you to pay a monthly amount into a special account from which bills will then be met. Banks make a small charge for this service but it can be very worthwhile and relieves you of one headache. Your bank budget account can also take care of other payments which do not have their own budget account system.

Once you have sorted out how you are going to pay for your utilities, you will need to work out how you can reduce your expenditure on them. Now is the time to 'Switch Off and Save'.

Cut down as much as possible on your lighting, heating and telephone bills. If you have children, enlist their help and get them to see it as a game. Encourage them to switch off unnecessary lights, not to leave the television set playing to empty rooms and to put on extra clothing rather than turning the heating up. Government subsidies for loft insulation may make this a good investment for some of your redundancy money. The telephone is a very expensive instrument, but try to keep it if you can. Without a telephone you can feel very cut off at a time when you most need the support of your friends and relatives. In addition a telephone is an indispensable aid for job hunting. To cut down on costs, start making your calls out of peak hours wherever possible and discourage your children from making lengthy calls to their friends. Fuel bills will escalate if you stay at home all day when the house has normally been empty, so try and spend part of the day out of the house. Much of your job hunting can be done outside the home and your local library is an ideal place to write job applications and to look up information on potential employers.

Job-Hunting Expenses

Job hunting is expensive not only because of buying newspapers in order to read the job ads but because of the cost of photocopying CVs and postage. Postage is something you will have to pay for yourself, but getting your CVs typed and photocopied is another area where your employer can help you. If your employer does not mention this, then ask. It is wise to get at least a hundred copies made in the first instance and ask your employer if he would be willing to do a few more for you at a later date if they are needed. Visits to the library will also enable you to read the job ads without buying the newspapers. Libraries get all the major dailies and a daily visit will ensure that you do not miss any job opportunities.

Job hunting can also be expensive from the travel point of view. Try and time your visits to agencies, Jobcentres and suchlike at off-peak travel times if you are going by public transport. When you arrange to attend an interview, ask politely whether the employer intends paying expenses. If not, then make sure the interview time coincides with the off-peak period. If there are no expenses and the job is outside your local area, your Jobcentre will be able to help you, providing it is not a high salary job. If you are likely to look for jobs outside your local area, ask for information about the financial help available under the 'Travel to Interview' Scheme when you first visit your Jobcentre and find out if you will be eligible for help. You have to apply before rather than after you attend the interview. You are eligible for help once you have been unemployed for four weeks and the scheme covers actual travel expenses plus overnight accommodation if this is necessary.

When you attend interviews with companies who agree to pay expenses, you will usually be asked to fill in an expenses form when you visit the company. If your interviewer forgets to mention expenses, then it is quite in order to ask politely, 'How do I claim for my expenses?' If you have the usual British inhibitions about talking about money, then write a letter afterwards to your interviewer thanking him for the interview and mentioning that you are looking forward to hearing further from him and enclosing a note of your expenses. Needless to say, these should be reasonable and not inflated expenses.

Loans and Hire-Purchase

Loan payments, like mortgage payments, can be rescheduled, but again it is important to let the appropriate organization know that you may have difficulties in repaying as soon as possible. Whatever you do, do not let anyone tempt you to take out another loan in order to cover payments for an existing loan. If you think you will face difficulties financially, they will only be compounded by attempting to ward off the evil moment of payment by further borrowing. The Citizens Advice Bureaux operate debt counselling services for people facing financial problems and if you think you are likely to experience problems you should seek their advice immediately.

Food

Food is an area where economies will usually need to be made. By economizing on food you can actually improve your and your family's health, so this need not cause any hardship. The requisites of a healthy diet are discussed further in Chapter 5, but the basic principles are to replace frozen and convenience foods with fresh food and to eat cheaper or less meat.

Leisure Expenses

Drink, cigarettes and entertainment are all areas where cutbacks will need to be made. Although from the practical point of view it is a good idea to give up smoking now your income is reduced, from a psychological point of view it may be the worst possible time to do this. In a stressful situation such as redundancy, it is not the ideal time to add more stress by attempting to give up smoking. What you must not do however, and this applies equally to drinking, is to increase your consumption.

Many leisure activities have special rates for unemployed people. Local authorities often have reduced admission charges for sporting facilities especially during weekdays when facilities may be under-utilized. This is not to suggest that you should spend all the time that you should be devoting to job hunting, playing tennis or squash or improving your backstroke instead, but concessions may boost your morale by allowing you to keep up an activity which you might not otherwise be able to afford. Theatres, cinemas and other cultural activities also often offer concessions to the unemployed.

If you have booked a holiday before finding out about your redundancy, you may have a difficult decision to make. Attractive though the idea of a break may be, if you are unemployed for any length of time, you may find yourself regretting all that money spent on beer and vino on the Costa del Sol when the bills are coming in. Many travel insurances now have a redundancy clause which will enable you to claim back whatever money you have put down, and if this is possible with yours, it is probably wise to take advantage of this. You can always put the money aside and if you get a job quickly then use it to have a last-minute two-week holiday before you start the new job. You will enjoy the holiday that much more if you know that you are going back to a job rather than to a place in the dole queue. If your insurance does not cover redundancy (and in today's economic climate everyone's should), you will have to decide whether or not to go ahead. If you are already fully paid up there may be little point in pulling out, but if you have paid only a deposit it may be best to pull out now rather than to throw good money after bad. Even if you are not covered by travel insurance, some travel companies will be sympathetic to your situation and may offer some kind of refund if you write to them.

If you are going on holiday in the UK, you can continue to receive benefit for a two-week period by filling in a holiday form at the Benefit Office, giving an address where you can be contacted if a job vacancy turns up. If however you take a holiday abroad, you are not considered 'available for work' and you will not be able to claim.

If you have been a regular attender of a social club, you may feel inclined once you are unemployed to hide yourself away and not go. In a club where drinking is involved you will want to avoid getting caught up in large-scale round-buying sessions, but try if you can to pop in for a short time once a week at least. It will not only boost your morale to keep in touch with your friends and prevent you sinking into the isolation which many unemployed people impose upon themselves, but it will remind them that you are still about and on the job market. A large percentage of jobs are obtained by word of mouth, through friends and acquaintances who have heard about jobs on the grapevine. Whilst acquaintances may not bother to ring you up to tell you about a job they have heard is going, they will certainly tell you if you bump into them when you are out and about. If you find it difficult to keep up your annual subscription, ask if they can reduce it. Redundancy is such a common occurrence now that you will certainly not be the first person to have asked and most social clubs will not want to lose you as a result of your being unemployed.

Clothing

For job hunting purposes you will need one and preferably two outfits which are clean, tidy and appropriate for the type of work you are seeking. Before you start your job search you will need to spend some money getting your job-hunting outfits cleaned, and if necessary mended, and your shoes repaired. Once you have got these outfits in good condition, keep them that way and if possible put them aside for job hunting only. The last thing you want is to receive a sudden summons for an interview only to find the heel of your shoe has fallen off and you have egg on the lapel of your interview suit. Once you have your interview outfits, cut back on clothes expenditure as much as possible and 'Make do and mend' as far as the rest of your clothes are concerned.

Cars

Together with housing and utilities costs, cars are the next major source of outlay. With your redundancy money it is a good idea to make sure that any essential servicing and repairs are carried out and that your tax and insurance are paid up for the year ahead. This means that you will not need to worry about keeping your car on the road while you are job hunting. If you have had a company car, your company may let you keep it for a time while you are job hunting. Alternatively they may allow you to buy the car at a cheap rate and this could be a good investment for part of your redundancy money. If nothing is mentioned about the car when you are told about your redundancy, then these are points to consider when negotiating your severance package. If you have ever thought about evening classes in car maintenance, now might be the time to start.

Subscriptions to Clubs and Professional Bodies

Many professionals whose qualifications are essential to their employment will have to maintain their subscriptions to their professional bodies. In some cases, such as the British Institute of Management, if membership is allowed to lapse, you will need to start the application process afresh when you rejoin and will have to pay a new entry fee. Many such memberships include the associations' magazines and journals which may be one of the major sources of jobs in some occupations and it will be essential to continue receiving these. Many bodies now have special rates for those unemployed and if you are anticipating having to renew subscriptions during your period of unemployment, then write to the membership secretary advising him or her of your circumstances and asking if there are any special arrangements. Do not be inhibited about this. The organization concerned will certainly not want to lose membership because people have to drop out through temporary financial embarrassment.

If you have tended to be rather a non-participating member of such organizations, it is worthwhile, now that you are unemployed and have more time, to start attending monthly meetings and similar functions as they can be invaluable sources of job contacts. If your employer has previously paid your subscription, this is something where you could ask him to help out, particularly if you are expecting to have to renew membership shortly after your redundancy.

The items mentioned above are just a guide on how to cut your expenditure rather than an exhaustive list, and each individual will have to carefully examine his or her own budget. The most difficult area for economy is not however the money we spend on ourselves, but the money we spend on our children. Telling your horse-mad 8-year-old that you can no longer afford riding lessons or your 10-year-old would-be soccer star that you can no longer afford football match tickets is going to make you feel as popular as Saddam Hussein, but you may have to do it. Tell your children exactly why you are having to make economies. If you are honest with them and explain the situation fully, they will be much more understanding. Try and see if there are any ways of allowing them to keep up their activities. If your child is a member of a school football team, you have probably been used to paying his fare to Saturday games, but schools will often have a fund for the fares of children whose parents cannot pay, so write a letter to the teacher and explain the position. Similarly, with other school expenses such as school trips and ingredients for cookery classes, there is often provision for those who cannot afford them.

Some children can be more enterprising at wringing concessions out of the system than their parents. One parent of our acquaintance, after scrimping and saving to pay for her son's school camping trip, was surprised to receive a telephone call a month beforehand from the school secretary to let her know that her son's holiday grant had come through. When she replied somewhat surprisedly that she hadn't applied for a grant, she was informed that her son had applied on his own initiative because he'd said his mum couldn't afford it.

Your children may be able to keep up their hobbies by paying or working their own way. Stables will often provide free riding in return for helping out and children can earn themselves additional pocket money by getting a paper round or offering to wash neighbours' cars or mow their lawns. If you are on a low income you may also qualify for other state benefits such as free school meals, free prescriptions and free school uniform which may help with your expenses. Details of these are obtainable from Social Security offices.

The strategy for all expenses, your own and your children's, must be to economize innovatively. Do not draw the lace curtains and sit at home brooding, but be open about your temporarily diminished finances and see how far people are willing to go to help you. In most cases it will be further than you think.

Chapter 3
The Job Search

The initial reaction to being made redundant varies between people. It depends on how the news was broken and how expected it was. A key factor is the personality of the individual concerned and how this links in with the domestic situation, on-going commitments and how the ease or difficulty of finding a new job is regarded. After the shock often comes a sense of relief, a sense of freedom. You have a lump sum payment, you're home, free from the rat race and now you can do everything you ever wanted to do. The first few weeks can seem like a holiday, a bonus, and the days pass enjoyably doing all those odd jobs and driving around on pleasant day trips. After all you deserve a break and you can look for jobs later. For others this optimistic stage will be very short-lived and they will quickly move into a sense of helplessness and moody despair; wasting the days in brooding and black melancholy, too depressed to start the job-hunting process. Exaggerated extremes? Possibly, but also possessing more than a grain of truth.

Job hunting and finding the best possible job can be a long and time-consuming process. It is absolutely essential to get the whole process under way as soon as possible. If you are feeling down, doing something constructive is the best way to climb out of that. If you're feeling up, use that confidence positively by getting things moving. Now is not the time to busy yourself around the house. Now is the time to plant the seeds for your future.

Most people, from all walks of life, either overestimate or underestimate their abilities. Having just been made redundant, the majority are inclined to underestimate themselves seriously. Start positively. Get to know yourself better by drawing up lists of your strengths. Divide them up between personal skills and achievements. Personal skills can be further divided between those relating to your personality (energetic, industrious, ambitious, conscientious etc.) and those skills you have acquired (professional qualifications, use of certain equipment, knowledge of languages, computer experience) through training, education and work experience.

Look at what you have done well in your past career over and above the accepted responsibilities of whatever job you held. Hitting production targets, winning that important overseas contract, retooling that lathe. Whatever you know you have done well, put it down. Now do exactly the same with your weaknesses. This isn't designed to get you depressed, but to get you to look at your shortcomings realistically and to take a positive approach to them. Look at them again and work out ways of overcoming these weaknesses and avoiding making the same mistakes again.

Take heart from this exercise. We're willing to bet that the positives, once you start thinking about them, will easily outnumber the negatives. Used constructively this list will prove to be most useful to you during the job hunt. Firstly it creates confidence – based on a realistic assessment of your abilities rather than on euphoria. Secondly it will be a useful reference point when you're asked to complete that section of application forms marked 'Give here any points of special relevance to this appointment.' You can simply pick out the relevant ones. Thirdly, at interview, you will often be asked to describe your strengths and weaknesses. How to handle that question is dealt with at length in Chapter 4, but your list will give you a basis for your reply.

What to Apply For

For the majority of people who have had redundancy thrust on them the question of what types of job to apply for is easily solved. They will simply want to get back in at the same level in a similar sphere or, perhaps, if things go well, a slightly more senior position, again in a similar environment. Some people however will use redundancy as a means to making a complete break in their career path, a point for a new departure, and we will be examining this in Chapter 8.

For most, as we have said, the issue is clear-cut. A sales rep in, for example, bathroom fittings, will continue to look for similar positions or perhaps look one rung higher up, at the field sales or sales manager level. Should this person just look at other bathroom fittings manufacturers, or can the net be cast wider?

With this particular instance it is reasonable to assume that in the lists of strengths and achievements this person has compiled, contacts with retailers and wholesalers will come pretty high on the list. Selling, after all, is the art of having the right product at the right price and time for the right people. Who are these people? What else apart from bathroom fittings do they buy? What other product areas are they interested in? Which other companies, therefore, in different fields but selling to the same buyer, would be interested in having someone with these contacts working for them? This is a simple, and perhaps obvious example, but it shows that, given a little thought surrounding your own strengths and particular areas of knowledge and experience, you can perhaps widen significantly the types and number of positions to apply for – and thus significantly increase your chance of a job.

How to Find Jobs

Where do you find these jobs, and how, in competition with over two million unemployed, do you get offered them? The truth is that although unemployment remains distressingly high, a newly redundant person has tremendous advantages over the vast majority of the unemployed. Firstly, skills and experience have been acquired, and secondly, proof of a recent sound employment record is a much more bankable asset than an equivalent record fast receding in the mists of time.

Ignoring internal promotions, which hopefully create new opportunities lower down the scale, jobs are filled predominantly through three main channels: advertising, agencies and consultancies, and word of mouth. For ease of exposition we will treat each separately, although many jobs are filled using a combination of two or even all three methods.

Answering Job Advertisements

Using national, local and specialized trade press relevant to your particular area, industry and occupation, a picture will start to emerge of the type, number and scope of the opportunities available to you. Most specialist trade and professional publications are either weekly or monthly and are often bought by companies and circulated around the office. They can take up to a month to reach those at the bottom of the circulation list and job advertisers will expect responses to trickle in over a period of a few weeks. Because of this time lag, it is worthwhile going through the back issues of publications at your local library. Who knows that you won't find a suitable opening in one of the most recent back issues? Generally speaking, the more senior the position the longer it takes to fill. If a consultancy is handling an assignment it may take four to six weeks from the appearance of the ad before they can present a shortlist to the client company. It is therefore worth applying if you are still within that time scale.

The most important things to consider when applying are: whether; 1, it is a job you could do; 2, it is a job you could convince an employer/consultant that you could do; and 3, it fits your requirements in terms of salary levels and location.

These factors won't all be positive in all jobs you see. It is however worthwhile spreading the net a little wider especially if you have not been through the job-hunting exercise previously – or at least for a very long time. If the job sounds right but is in the wrong place or the salary isn't quite what you were looking for, apply for it anyway. Similarly, if it's a job you'd like to do but think it might be difficult persuading others that you could – still apply. It could lead to other things developing and it's worth it to get some professional interview practice. In short, when in doubt put the ball firmly into the employer's court.

Initially it is unwise to be too discriminating in your job

applications. Until you have tested the waters, you may find it difficult to gauge exactly for which jobs you will obtain interviews. Many people either overestimate or underestimate their attractiveness to future employers and will apply for jobs for which they are over- or under-qualified. In neither case are they likely to succeed in obtaining interviews. Particularly if you are uncertain about the type of job you should seek, it is a good idea to apply for a range of jobs and see which ones result in immediate rejections and which ones get taken further. This will give you an idea of your market value and where you should be pitching yourself on the job market. Even if you do obtain interviews for jobs which you ultimately decide are not for you, you will have had some interview practice. Knowing that you don't want the job, you can relax at the interview, enjoy selling yourself and hone up on your technique.

There are definite advantages in applying for jobs on a fairly open-minded basis when you first start job hunting and in attending interviews in order to get interview practice. There are however some disadvantages. One of these relates to the fact that you may perform well at interviews for jobs which you don't want because you will seem relaxed and appear confident. This may result in your being offered jobs which you don't want, and at the initial stages of job hunting this can involve some difficult decisions. If you have been unemployed for some time, it may be necessary to take a job that is not really you in order to get back into employment, but if you have not been unemployed for very long it can be difficult to know what decision to make. Dealing with unwanted job offers is covered further in Chapter 7.

Another disadvantage of applying for jobs which you would like to do, but for which your experience is not quite right, is that you will receive a high proportion of rejections for such jobs. This can be demoralizing even though rationally you know you were 'kite flying'. It is still a good idea to apply for the jobs which you would like to have as well as those you are likely to be able to get, but you should make a clear distinction in your mind between the two. When applying decide which category the particular job fits and if it is not one where your background is very appropriate but one where you feel you could sell yourself to the employer if given a chance, you need not feel too disappointed if the company decides to play safe and to go for an apparently safer bet. Monitor carefully for which types of jobs you get interviews and which types of jobs seem to be outside your scope. This will enable you to channel your energies in the most productive directions.

One of the Unemployment Research Unit's findings was that employers frequently complained about the lack of discrimination shown by unemployed people in applying for jobs. As one Recruitment Officer put it:

> *Unemployed people are getting more desperate. They're applying for jobs that they're not suited to. Definitely. I get people, I had one the other day and he said this was the fiftieth position he'd applied for in two months and this was the first interview he'd got. But all those fifty jobs, they can't all be relevant to him; they can't.*

If you apply for a job outside your normal range, you must sell yourself to the employer at both the application stage and at the interview if there is one. Just wanting *a* job is not considered a sufficient reason by employers for applying. Employers want you to be interested in their particular company and their particular job. This may necessitate rewriting your job experience to highlight areas of experience in your previous jobs so they appear relevant to the job you are seeking. You may be applying on the basis that you have done activities related to the job on a voluntary basis or through some social activity. You have always worked in a factory but would like a job as a sales rep. How can you gear your background to what the employer wants? Examine your background. Your factory experience will have given you certain product knowledge which could put you in a good position to sell that type of product. You may not have worked as a salesman, but may have sold raffle tickets for your local social club and succeeded in upping sales. You may have been a voluntary bingo caller at your local hospital and so acquired 'the gift of the gab'. If you want to make a non-run-of-the-mill job change, spell out to the employer why you are suitable, don't expect them to read between the lines and work it out for themselves. They simply do not have the time.

When you do come to apply for jobs, do make sure that you follow the instructions given in each ad. If they ask you to telephone, do not write instead. If they ask you to send in a CV, do that. If they ask you to request an application form, don't send them a CV instead. It's all basic common sense. Don't give them an opportunity to overlook you purely on a technicality.

About CVs

No two people will ever agree on what constitutes a perfect CV. In the following pages we have given some examples together with a sample covering letter. The CVs vary in the type of person and career described and thus the level of position sought, but they all follow the same basic format and follow certain rules. Use them as a rough model on which to develop your own.

1. Be Brief
The person reading your CV will be busy and thus unwilling to read through pages of detail. A good CV should summarize the essential features about you and your career. An outline which carries sufficient weight for an informed decision to be made is the ideal to aim for. The detail – the whys, hows and wherefores – can be developed at the interview.

2. Personal Details
Again put down the minimum. It's surprising how much detail some people think essential to put down on their CV. Such things as height, weight, wife's maiden name, father's occupation and the fact that you play the organ are very rarely going to help you get a job. Where possible avoid putting down facts which have to be updated such as your own age and those of your children. Stick to date of birth only.

3. Career Details
Show all relevant jobs in reverse chronological order. Generally your most recent job is the one which is going to be the most significant in terms of level attained, seniority and relevance to the position you are seeking, so

it makes sense to get that square on the front page. It will have more impact than a list of training courses or junior jobs spanning two decades. Similarly, make sure that the dimensions of the job are clearly stated. 'Marketing Director' is a title indicating a level of responsibility, but the size of company in which you had this job will obviously have a bearing on the true level of responsibility. For more senior jobs, list your *achievements* as well as your responsibilities in order to give the person reading your CV some evidence of your ability and thus a reason to see you.

4. Salary and Career Objectives

We prefer keeping these off the CV, although there are valid arguments for their inclusion. Our view is that the CV should be as multi-purpose a document as possible. Listed objectives in the CV limit the scope of positions for which you can apply unless you make them all-embracing and therefore over-generalized. Similarly with salary, companies hate too wide a variance between what you were earning and what they are offering. You might find yourself ruled out before an interview purely on that discrepancy. Objectives and salary are best dealt with in a covering letter which is geared towards that particular job opportunity. Here too you can bring out aspects of your career particularly relevant to that job which might not appear on a short CV. Although temptingly time-saving, don't print hundreds of all-purpose covering letters with gaps to fill in as applicable. It gives the impression that you are indiscriminate in your job hunting when all employers want to believe that you particularly want to work for *them*. If your past salary relates to what is on offer, mention it in the letter; if not, leave it off. You can talk about salary at interview.

Finally the purpose of the CV is to secure a meeting. It is a selling document. If in doubt about how much to include, go for less rather than more. Excite their curiosity and make them want to see you.

Should one stretch the truth at all? It would be totally stupid to claim levels of responsibilities or achievements which you hadn't in fact attained. People would soon see through you at interview and once trust had gone the person concerned would do anything to avoid employing you, no matter how suitable you might otherwise be. Similarly with the actual career progression; don't rationalize it in terms of job progressions, companies worked for and dates. These facts are easily verifiable and will be the first thing checked when references are taken.

What can be improved however is the way these facts are assembled, marshalled and presented. If you were after a sales job for example, it would make sense not only to emphasize the previous sales jobs you had held but also, if you held positions within other functions – marketing, production, finance or whatever – to bring out the links you had with sales within those functions and to emphasize how that grounding enabled you to sell better by understanding the other aspects of the business and the inter-relation of these functions with sales. All this would be perfectly true but perhaps not realized by the person reading your CV unless pointed out.

This leads to the question of whether it is wise to prepare different CVs for the different job areas for which one might wish to apply. This is very difficult to give a definite yes or no to, depending as it does on the breadth of experience you as an individual have attained. With most people the accumulation of their experience and the thrust of their job progression will lead them to a fairly narrow band of types of job for which to apply. The CV can therefore be standard with particularly relevant aspects of experience related to a specific job brought out more fully in a covering letter.

Curriculum Vitae

JENNIFER BROWN

Address:	52 Dallington Road Havant Hants
Telephone:	(06892) 56743
Date of Birth:	11.2.48
Marital Status:	Married, two independent children
Education:	Norwich Grammar School Portsmouth Technical College 1975-76, one-year secretarial course. Obtained RSA III Typewriting, RSA II Shorthand (with distinction), RSA II Secretarial Studies, RSA II Audio-typing

Career:

1990 to date   *PERSONNEL ASSISTANT/SECRETARY*
Marine Supply Co. (UK) Limited, 214 Old
Road, Havant, Hants. Yacht supply
company.
Responsible to Personnel Director for all
personnel administration matters for staff
of 180, recruitment of clerical and
secretarial staff including writing and
placing of job advertisements, liaising
with agencies and initial interviewing.
Also acted as confidential secretary to
Personnel Director. Recruited firstly as
Secretary to Finance Manager and
promoted after 18 months.

1986-90   *SECRETARY*
Lee & Smith Ltd, 100 Soton Road,
Portsmouth, Hants. Marine Engineers.
Responsible for all secretarial work for
Marketing Department of 5. Drafted own

correspondence, arranged client presentations and buffet lunches, organized overseas travel arrangements and maintained small library of press cuttings.

Other Information:	I am a car owner-driver. My current secretarial speeds are shorthand 120 wpm, typing and audio-typing 70 wpm.
Previous Employment:	Prior to 1985 I was a full-time housewife. My early work experience was as a children's nanny in private households.

Curriculum Vitae

GERALD SANDERS

Address: 3 The Moorings
              Old Canal Lane
              Coventry
              CV1 7XX

Telephone: (0223) 98152

Date of Birth: 4.8.45

Marital Status: Married, two children

Education: Ealing Secondary Modern School

Career:

1985 to present *FOREMAN*
              Arthur Stewart & Co. Ltd, 49 The High
              Street, Guildford, Surrey. Civil Engineers.
              Responsible for supervision of
              construction work on 5 different projects:
              ● Coventry Shopping Centre
              ● The Grange Housing Estate, Nuneaton
              ● Milton Keynes Shopping Centre
              ● Maidstone By-pass
              ● Daventry Ring Road

1984-85   *FOREMAN*
              Bernard Moon & Sons Ltd, 129-133
              Warwick Road, Coventry. Civil Engineers.
              Employed on Daventry Ring Road project.

1980-84   *FOREMAN*
              William Forsythe & Co. Ltd, Forsythe
              House, Great West Road, Brentford, Middx.
              Civil Engineers.
              Employed on Isle of Grain Power Station
              project, initially as Ganger, promoted after
              one year to Foreman supervising heavily
              unionized labour force.

53

1978-80   *FOREMAN*
           Bernard Moon & Sons Ltd, (as above)
           Employed on Abu Dhabi airport extension
           project working in temperatures of up to
           130°F with a largely Pakistani workforce.

Previous   Prior to 1978 I was employed by various
Experience: civil engineering companies on projects in
            the UK and Middle East.

Other   I speak some Arabic and Urdu and am a
Information: car owner-driver. I would be prepared to
             work anywhere in the UK or overseas on
             either single or married status.

Curriculum Vitae

ALEX GARDNER

Address: 13 Cerridwen Crescent
Avebury
Wilts
SN4 9EW

Telephone: Avebury (0988) 777

Date of Birth: 21 June 1949

Marital Status: Married, three children

Education: 1968-71: Exeter University
BA(Hons) English Literature 2:1
1961-68: Ampleforth Priory
3 'A' levels: English(A), History(B),
Economics(C)
9 'O' levels

Professional Member: British Institute of Management
Qualifications: Member: Institute of Marketing

Additional Marketing: principles and practice:
Training: Cranfield, 2 weeks; Basics of General
Management: Henley, 1 week

Career:
1985 to date *Hutchinson Wilkes PLC*
The Company specializes in the
manufacture and sale of a wide range of
branded food products. Current turnover
c.£100m employing 2,000 on 3 sites in the
UK.

1989 to date *MARKETING DIRECTOR*
Reporting to the Chief Executive,
responsibilities include the overall
planning and marketing strategy for 4
distinct product areas: biscuits, chocolate

bars, sugar confectionery and preserves.
In addition, control advertising and new
product development budgets: annual
spend £3.75m. Staff directly reporting =
5:3 Marketing Managers, Product
Development Manager and Advertising
Manager, and through them a team of 40.
Achievements include:

- overall sales increasing from £80m to
  £100m in 2 years
- increased profitability of sugar
  confectionery ranges from 15 per cent
  to 23 per cent gross margin
- successful launch of preserves product
  ranges into France capturing 3 per
  cent of market in first 6 months.

1985-89   *MARKETING MANAGER: BISCUITS*
Responsibilities included overall
promotion of biscuit ranges under 'True
Grit' label. In conjunction with New
Product Department successfully
launched new range of 'home-made'
natural biscuits under 'Granny's Own'
brand capturing 30 per cent of market in
first year after launch. Worked closely
with advertising agency on this
promotion with £1m product launch
spend.

1980-85   *Farley-Beers Ltd*
Subsidiary of Hardcastle Inc. specializing
in the manufacture and sale of household
appliances, fixtures, and fittings.
Turnover £5m. Workforce 600.

MARKETING MANAGER
Reporting to the Marketing Director. This
was a new appointment, the
responsibilities of which were to create a
coherent marketing strategy for the
company.

Achievements included:
- assessing profitability of over 400 different product lines
- cutting out 150 of these lines which were making losses
- researching market to establish areas which could be developed by enhancing existing product range
- increasing overall profitability on total range by 17 per cent while turnover grew by 10 per cent.

1977-85   *Abbersley, Dwight, Wretch & Drew*
Advertising Agency
ACCOUNT DIRECTOR
Joined as Account Executive working on dog food and cat food accounts.
Promoted in 1980 to Account Manager to work on Deosil Oil's corporate advertising campaign. Total advertising spend £1.5m. Made Account Director in 1982 for the Hardcastle Inc. account to develop a corporate identity for their engineered products.

1975-76   Took 12-month sabbatical to see the world. Travelled overland to Australia and back via California.

1971-75   *Praxos and Gimble*
Multinational Company
PRODUCT MANAGER
Joined initially as Management Trainee, spending 6 months each in Production, Accounts, Marketing and Purchasing departments. Joined New Product Department on 'Zilch', the new bio-digestible washing powder. Promoted in 1974 to head up small team working on detergent-impregnated disposable wash cloths.

Covering Letter

13 Cerridwen Crescent
Avebury
Wilts
30 April 1992

Joseph E Brown Esq.
Managing Director
Diablo Chocolates Ltd
Diablo House
Cocoa Lane
Kettering
Northants

Dear Mr Brown

I wish to apply for the position of Marketing Director
which you advertise in today's edition of *The Sunday
Times*.

I enclose a copy of my curriculum vitae. From this you will
see that for the last three years I have had overall
responsibility for the direction and development of the
Hutchinson Wilkes chocolate bar range. During my tenure,
sales in this sector rose by more than 15 per cent and I
oversaw three successful product launches.

My previous experience has given me a wide
understanding of all aspects of marketing branded
consumer goods and consumer appliances. My six years in
advertising were especially useful in gaining an
understanding of how to create 'brand awareness' in a
highly competitive market sector.

Following the proposed takeover of Hutchinson Wilkes by
White Knight Industries, I am now looking for a new
career challenge. I am very attracted to your position
which I see as an ideal opportunity to develop my
marketing skills in a fast-growing sector of the food
industry.

In addition to my experience in this field, I can offer hard
work, enthusiasm and a successful record in man-
management. I look forward to discussing my career with
you.

Yours sincerely

Alex Gardner

Where somebody has moved across the boundaries of
specific functions as part of their career progression, having
spent several years, for example, in each of the financial,
production and marketing functions and feels equally
competent to do a job in any of these spheres, then it could
make sense to have three different CVs all containing the
same factual information but in the presentation and
interpretation of these facts bringing out the strengths and
relevance for each of the different disciplines. In most cases
however the covering letter will be sufficient to bring out
the relevance of a simple straightforward and clear CV.

We have mentioned the need to put dates by each
employment and against each position. What should you
do however when it comes to the most recent appointment?
Should you indicate your unemployed state to the
consultant or prospective employer? Bear in mind that even
though attitudes are changing to unemployment, it is much
more likely that you will gain a preliminary interview if the
interviewer assumes that you are still employed. It is sad
but true that there is still some prejudice in the minds of
employers against job applicants who are not currently in
employment. The more senior the job for which you are
applying, the more this is true. At the unskilled level it is
still commonplace for people to give up one job before
looking for another. Employers here are likely to be
comparing people with different lengths of unemployment
rather than people who are and are not unemployed. If you
are newly redundant, you will usually be in a very good
position for unskilled jobs and employers will prefer you
to those who have been unemployed for some time. The
higher up the occupational tree you go, the more likely you
are to be competing with those still in employment and the
more unemployment will weigh against you.

Employers' reasoning behind their prejudice against unemployed applicants has some valid and some less valid points. Some people still subscribe heavily to the Protestant Work Ethic and believe that it is somehow 'immoral' to be unemployed. Managers are much more immune to redundancy than other workers and despite the recent increase in managerial unemployment, few of those who are in the position of interviewing people have themselves been unemployed. Many such people find it difficult to understand that it can take someone a long time to find another job. This attitude is not valid in today's high unemployment situation and fortunately it is slowly on the decline.

There are, however, more valid reasons for employers' prejudices against the unemployed. As we have mentioned, unemployed people often apply for jobs for which they are unsuitable, and when they come for interviews, employers often find themselves confronted with anxious, bitter or despairing people whom they would rather avoid. You can however avoid falling into either of these traps. We have given you some ideas on how to sell yourself for a range of jobs. In the next chapter we will explain how you should present yourself at interview.

Certain managers are more receptive to unemployed applicants than others. Female managers are less prejudiced against the unemployed than male managers and you will stand a better chance with a female employer or interviewer. On the other hand you will find agencies and consultancies are more prejudiced against the unemployed than are employers themselves. Being intermediaries, they are in the position of acting rather like a marriage broker and selling the two parties, applicant and employer, to one another. In order to maintain their credibility agencies and consultancies will tend to play safe and screen out anyone they think may not be acceptable to their clients or who might reflect badly on them.

The existence of such prejudices has led some employers to keep redundant staff on their books and nominally employed for a period so that they can do their job hunting as an employee. This is something you may like to ask your employer to consider.

Getting Help From Your Last Employer

What help can your company give you in finding another job? The answer is potentially quite a lot if it is encouraged to do so. As soon as employees have been notified of redundancies, good employers will start contacting other firms in the area to inform them that they have some very good staff whom they are making redundant to see whether they may be interested. Often this will produce interviews even if the companies concerned were not actively recruiting. Through manpower planning exercises they may be aware of gaps in the workforce which are likely to appear in a few months' time through retirement or promotion and if they can earmark at no cost a replacement who comes recommended from a company they know well, they may take that person on in a designate position before the actual job gap appears. Managers, through local branches of organizations such as the British Institute of Management and Institute of Personnel Management, will be in touch with managers in many other companies in the area and a direct approach to friends and acquaintances can often secure someone a new job before one has left the old. If your employer is willing to approach other employers, ask them if they will give you a list of those contacted and the name of the contact and follow these up yourself. Where the initial contact has not produced any interviews then write a follow-up letter. The correct form for a business letter is given overleaf.

Even if you draw a blank with (in this example) Taylors Brushes, Mr Smith will know other Mr Smiths in other companies. If it comes up in conversation that they are looking for people with your experience, he may well recall having had a CV from you and pass your name on.

Once your employer has exhausted his contacts and you have followed them up, what other help can be given? Your Personnel Department can be a primary source of help. Your Personnel Manager is an expert on curriculum vitae, interview behaviour, letters of application and the correct media for different types of job advertisements. This is all knowledge which you need to acquire and you should ask your Personnel Manager for help and advice on the different aspects of job hunting. If a few of you are involved

5 Yew Tree Avenue
Hemel Hempstead
Herts
2 March 1992

A D Smith Esq.
Managing Director
Taylors Brushes Ltd
Valey Industrial Estate
Hoddesdon
Herts

Dear Mr Smith

My Personnel Manager, David Jones, has been in touch
with you recently about possible job vacancies with your
company. I understand from Mr Jones that you are not
anticipating any vacancies at present, but perhaps you
would bear me in mind for the future.

I enclose a copy of my curriculum vitae, which gives my
home address and telephone number.

Yours sincerely

C B Brown

in the redundancy, ask your Personnel Department if they could run a short course for all of you.

We will assume now that you have been successful in getting the ball rolling and that invitations for interviews are now coming through. The interviews could either be with consultancies or with companies and could be either to discuss specific jobs or be fairly relaxed affairs designed to enable them to put a face to your CV so they will know what sort of person you are when a future job opportunity comes up. Should you go to them even though the job itself doesn't sound too wonderful? Should you go when they have made it quite clear that they haven't got a specific job for you at that precise moment?

The answer to both questions has to be an emphatic yes. Your responsibility to yourself at this stage is to explore fully every lead and to maximize all opportunities. To answer the first question, the consultant or company who invites you in to discuss a low-level job might, on seeing you, realize your true capability and bear you in mind for better jobs they know are in the pipeline. Similarly, if they invite you in for a general chat, you can be fairly sure that they have hopes that there will be something positive coming up in the future for why else would they devote this time to you? Seize every opportunity in these early stages; cast your net as wide as possible to include as wide a range and choice of opportunities as possible. Later you might have some hard thinking to do about which opportunity to pursue, which job to take. But this is better than keeping your sights so narrow in these early stages that nothing crosses your range of vision for months on end.

Consultancies/Agencies

One of the few growth areas over the last decade has been the proliferation of private sector consultancies and agencies specially set up to help companies find the right people for specific opportunities and slots within their structures. They cover all areas of work from temporary manual labour to chief executives of major conglomerates.

What one has to remember is that they all exist to service companies who pay them fees, usually partly or wholly on a success-related basis. They are only going to be interested in you if you are likely to be of interest to their client companies. The trick, which we will explore later, is convincing them of this.

The types of employment agencies/consultancies can be broadly categorized into four main areas.

1. Jobcentres
Jobcentres deal primarily with less skilled jobs, but skilled jobs and managerial level appointments are also covered, so it is well worth looking at what they have to offer. No appointment is necessary, you just walk in and see what they have.

2. High Street Agencies
These specialize in low- to medium-skilled jobs. Their candidate base is gained mainly by people walking in off the street. They will interview as they come in and then match up with available vacancies. They are high-volume, small-fee businesses relying on speed of throughput for profit. They may specialize in particular industries or in functional areas such as secretarial/office, computer staff or junior accountancy.

3. Advertising and Executive Selection Consultancies
These specialize in medium to upper management bands. Candidates are found mainly by advertising each vacancy although they will often keep a register of all candidates who apply to use as a back-up to their advertising. Once the ad appears, the services vary according to the wishes (and recruitment budget) of their client company. They can range from acting purely as a post box – applications forwarded unopened – through to making recommendations (ranking) of the CVs to interviewing and drawing up a shortlist with detailed appraisals of each candidate. Fees are usually more expensive than the first category and usually involve a guaranteed element (even if only the cost of the advertisement). They don't usually specialize in specific industries although there is a growth of these dealing specifically in the computing and high-tech fields. The interview procedure is now, more likely than not, to involve psychometric testing. These can involve both ability tests and personality questionnaires.

4. Executive Search Consultancies

These consultancies very rarely advertise but rely instead on detailed network of contacts to recommend suitable people for senior positions. They are also known as headhunters. They will approach people direct who seem suitable for the particular position, these names being found by detailed research as well as through contacts. They will interview all suitable candidates or people they think might lead them to the right person. This is a time-intensive approach and thus much more expensive. A large part of their fee is paid on a retainer basis. Each assignment is handled with considerable care, usually taking 3 to 4 months or longer to complete.

Although I have mentioned the fee element, this is borne in each case purely by the companies who retain the consultancies' services. No charge should ever be made to candidates, and in fact consultancies are prohibited by statute from charging both the employer and prospective employee. A list of consultancies and agencies can be found at the back of this book.

Jobs up to Middle Management Level

Both jobcentres and high street agencies service a small local area and most of the jobs they handle will be confined to that area. If you are prepared to relocate, then frankly it is better to visit the agencies within each of your chosen areas rather than rely on any kind of inter-branch exchange.

Jobcentres operate a self-help system which means they pin up all their vacancies and generally do their best to keep them up to date. They are grouped under occupational types and it doesn't take too long to see if there is anything likely to interest you. If there is, you take a note of the details and have a brief interview with one of the staff who is dealing with that particular opportunity. Remember, apart from filling the vacancy their responsibilities and loyalties are with the prospective employer so they will try and deflect your interest if they don't think you are suitable. It is therefore up to you to convince them that you are. How to sell yourself – for this is what it really amounts to – we will deal with at length in a later chapter.

Let us however assume that you have been successful in

this. They will usually try to arrange an immediate meeting between you and the employer which will involve telephoning them and describing you over the phone and in your hearing. If the company think you sound OK, the telephone will be thrust at you and you will suddenly find yourself being interviewed over the phone. Be prepared for this, for a lot hangs on it. If you can sound confident, eager and yet relaxed, no mean feat, you'll almost certainly get an interview. Of course not all company/candidate meetings can be arranged so easily. You will know from experience how seldom one can reach a particular individual first time over the phone, but do be prepared for it. Indications of uncertainty or irresolution could put paid to your chances.

The procedure is much the same in the high street agencies. They differ however in not putting all their vacancies on display, but in putting just a selection of the more attractively paid ones on day-glo boards stuck on the window in much the same way as supermarkets advertise their special offers. Don't be too surprised however if the one in the window which sounds exactly right for you has just been filled. Their procedure is to interview you and firstly see if you match up to any of their current vacancies. If you do, then like the jobcentres they will be fast. So again, be prepared. If you don't match up to their current vacancies but they regard you as an employable prospect, they will ring around their clients to see if they can slot you in somewhere. In this sense therefore the high street agency is unique amongst the categories we've mentioned in that they will, in certain circumstances, promote your interests as a means of serving their own. If however you are not suitable for their type of vacancy or their type of client, they will make it abundantly clear. At this level of the employment market it does help to have a thick skin.

We are moving up the employment scale once the agency starts referring to itself as a consultancy, and to its staff as consultants as distinct from interviewers. Consultancies, according to their specialization, will cover the whole sweep of employment opportunities from middle management to the most senior levels.

Middle and Senior Management Consultancies

The method of approach that you should adopt to get the best out of the middle and senior management consultancies, whether they advertise or rely on headhunting, is totally and diametrically opposed to that which was put forward earlier in regard to the high street agencies. These consultancies organize themselves in a very different way and the last thing they want is unexpected callers interrupting their work plan. Call on them personally without an appointment and, should you be successful in breaking the defensive ramparts of receptionists and secretaries, you will be regarded with all the enthusiasm normally reserved for foot-in-the-door salesmen. In short they won't appreciate your keenness but will resent your intrusion. So this is not the best way to enlist their help.

All the senior consultancies will keep a register of potential candidates who write in to them direct. How well-organized this is and how much reliance is put on it varies greatly between the individual concerns. By and large if the consultancy fills most of its appointments through advertising, they are likely to regard their register as an emergency back-up for use if the ad hasn't produced the right result. Alternatively they may use the register for quick assignments with well-established clients who will ask them to check through their files before committing themselves to an advertising budget. Realistically speaking one is approaching this type of consultancy on the mail-shot principle; if your coverage is comprehensive enough, someone somewhere out there will be handling an assignment suitable for someone with your experience.

Headhunters, or Executive Search Consultants, are again inclined to regard things slightly differently. They will discourage personal callers but may regard your CV as a potential reference point for them. That is however a rather different prospect from regarding you as a potentially placeable candidate. They may well be much more interested in what you can tell them about your industry, your company and even the people working there. Should they have clients in that particular sector, they might well invite you in for a general chat ostensibly to discuss your future but in reality to find out as much as they can about who are the rising stars in your company or industry. Of course if you look good on paper and you are in a field where they have clients, they might then wish to see you anyway in your own right. It could be that they are currently handling, or expect to handle in the near future, an opportunity which fits your profile. If this is the case they will regard you as a potential candidate and interview you accordingly. We have put it this way round however because this is the order of greatest likelihood.

An even greater likelihood in both cases is that you will just get a polite standard acknowledgement that they are keeping your CV on file. This is to be expected and you mustn't be downhearted by it. A consultant who specializes in advertised assignments will probably handle between twenty and thirty distinct opportunities a year; an executive search consultant perhaps only half that number. Although some selection and search firms are very well-known and have international connections; each particular office is unlikely to have more than about half a dozen full-time consultants on their staff. It doesn't take much arithmetic and simple common sense to work out that the chances of any one consultant, given the immense breadth of job opportunities which exist, handling an assignment which is exactly right for you at the precise moment that you send in your CV are exceedingly small.

Yet consultancies account for the majority of recruitment exercises. How this is reconciled to the small number of job opportunities handled by individual consultants is through the tremendously large number of consultancies which have sprung up over the last decade and, in particular, over the last ten years. It is a fragmented market with no one consultancy having over 5 per cent market share, although in specific industries and functions this percentage would be much higher. It is important therefore that you, as a job-seeker, get as wide a coverage as possible amongst all these consultancies (most of the better-known ones are listed in Chapter 9), get your CV on their files and then ensure that you get remembered by them.

Yet how is this achieved, given that their loyalties are predominantly to their client companies? And how does

Prepare CV and
brief covering letter
suggesting meeting

Send it to as many
reputable consultancies
as you can find

See Chapter 9 for list,
use reference books to
augment. Phone
switchboard to get name
of individual

Await replies

Reply 1
'Sorry nothing to
interest you at present
but next time you
are near arrange to
meet for a chat'

Reply 2
'Yes, we have
something to
interest you'

Reply 3
'Thank you nothing
suitable at present, but
we will keep you on
file'

Reply 4
They don't respond

Action
Make sure you will be
passing that way.
Arrange meeting
through consultant's
secretary. Use duo
positive alternative
(see below)

Action
Arrange interview
regardless of
apparent suitability
of job

Action
After 2 or 3 weeks,
phone to see whether
situation has changed.
Suggest chat using duo
positive alternative
(see below)

If yes

If no
Wait a while. Don't
pester them. Use a
book to justify your
call, e.g.
(a) change in situation
(b) widened area of job
search
(c) wider geographical
area
(d) broader salary
range
Suggest meeting to
discuss the change.

If yes

If no
Remember you can't win
them all. If they are
this resistant to seeing
you then
(a) it is not worth
alienating them by
pushing harder,
(b) it sounds unlikely
that they handle jobs
appropriate to your
background and skills

Action
Phone to see if they
have received CV

If yes
Suggest meeting,
using duo positive
alternative (see below)

If no
Send new CV indicating
you will phone
in a few days
to
(a) make sure it has
arrived.
(b) arrange to meet

Action
Make sure you do
phone when you said
you would

Treat as

THE INTERVIEW

(See Chapter 4)

Note: Duo-Positive Alternative
The question 'Can you see me on
Wednesday afternoon?', leaves you
open to the response. 'No'. It is
better put as, 'I will be in your area
on Wednesday afternoon and also
for some of Thursday. Which
would be more convenient for you
to see me? By inviting them to
choose, you are gaining their
commitment to see you and also
making it more difficult for them to
refuse.

How to deal with Consultancies

one get remembered by them positively rather than, as can so easily happen, as a pain in the neck? As in most things the answer lies in the method of presentation rather than the substance itself. Remember you will have to package yourself in the most positive and attractive way possible in order to stand out from the competition. From the preparation of your CV to the final interview and job offer, presentation is the area which offers you the greatest scope for improvement. The substance: your work record, experience and skills are absolute in that they are verifiable and thus have to be accepted as they are. How they are presented however can make all the difference between an interview granted or not granted, a place on the shortlist or near miss, a job offer instead of coming second. The flow chart above outlines the approach to take with consultancies.

The key elements of the procedure are clearly the preparation of the initial CV with its accompanying letter plus the actual interview itself. Both are clearly critical and it is worthwhile spending some time getting these right.

We have examined advertising and consultancies as ways of finding a new position and they are, if you like, the formal structure which exists to get companies the right people to fill the right slots. What other ways are there which you can usefully develop which could lead you to the right position? The answer is really provided by two further questions: who would you like to work for and who knows you're looking?

Who Would You Like to Work For: The Direct Approach

Consultancies and agencies don't of course create jobs; they merely handle vacancies which occur in companies who are perhaps too busy to take on the whole of the recruitment exercise themselves. They, the companies, are often thinking about taking on extra people for specific slots long before they are handed to a consultancy or otherwise see the light of day. Writing to a company purely on a speculative basis may seem rather a shot in the dark – after all, unless you have inside knowledge there is no way of predicting which companies are considering recruitment at the exact time relevant to your application. Nonetheless a great number of job offers are made to people who have written to companies in this way. In fact, surveys such as the Policy Studies Institute's National Survey of the Unemployed have shown that 21 per cent of jobs are found through approaching employers direct.

Out of all the companies which exist, how do you choose which ones to send your CV? In practice the choice isn't as difficult as it seems as you will automatically be limited to certain parameters. You will need to ask the following questions:

- Which companies have the level of appointment I'm looking for?
- Which of these are in related fields to my own and therefore would be particularly interested in the skills and experience that I have amassed?
- Which of these are based in my local area or which have bases in areas I am prepared to relocate to?
- Which of these are successful and who are therefore more likely to be recruiting and less likely to make me redundant later?

You will probably find this simple checklist will reduce the choice to manageable proportions. Obviously if you are somebody who is prepared to work anywhere for anybody and you have a skill which is universally required, for example, an accountancy qualification, you might still find the list too long. But by applying your preferences you could probably reduce it to about twenty first choices, twenty second choices and so on. You could then approach these companies on a timed programme basis.

How do you make your approach? Should you telephone or write? By and large it is almost always better to write than to phone. Phone calls have a habit of coming through just at the moment when the person is preoccupied with something else. It is also very difficult to précis a lifetime's experience into a brief call, the usual result being hurried, garbled and not carrying its deserved weight. Always write – but keep it brief. The person it's addressed to will be busy and will decide in a maximum of two minutes whether to take things further or not. If you haven't communicated within that time frame you're lost. There is no right or wrong phrasing of course but we give an example of what might be expected. Don't stick to it slavishly however but change it around and develop it to suit your own individual style.

Who should it be addressed to? This really depends on what kind of appointment you're going for. Generally speaking the personnel manager/director in a medium to large company will be involved with recruitment up to middle manager level. If you are going for a more senior appointment or if you're applying to a company whose size may not warrant a personnel department, address it to the Managing Director. It's a case again of doing your homework. Telephone their switchboard or use the reference books to see whether they have a personnel department and, whatever else you may do at whichever level you decide to approach, find out the name of the individual holding the appropriate position. Never send a 'Dear Sir' letter to the Chief Executive of XYZ Company. Find out the appropriate individual's name and mark it for their personal attention. They are quite likely to assume that if you can't be bothered to find out even this basic information about them they needn't be too bothered about you.

Reference books which you will find useful are *Kompass*, the register of UK companies published under the auspices of the CBI, and various trade and industry directories. *Kompass* gives names, addresses, telephone numbers, products and senior personnel of companies. It comes in two volumes, one which lists companies under geographical location and another which lists them by their product or service. You can thus identify companies in particular industries and particular areas where you would like to work. Trade and industry directories will give additional companies to those in *Kompass* and some will also give key company personnel. Reference books can be found in your local reference library and also in the libraries of professional bodies and trade associations. These tend to be based in London or other large cities, but you may find it worthwhile to take a day trip and spend the day in the library locating potential employers.

Usually companies are responsive to this type of approach. A relevant CV and a positive approach in your letter will impress them, as will the fact that you are doing something constructive about your situation. Obviously they cannot see everyone who writes in, and they may not have a suitable opening at that particular moment, but it could well lead to something. Should they offer you the chance of a general discussion, jump at it. You have nothing to lose and something could develop from that meeting.

Who Knows You are Looking: Networking

A common reaction to redundancy is to lose confidence in yourself and your abilities and to feel a sense of shame in your situation. You may feel that you wish to avoid people, but this is totally the wrong attitude to take and will cut you off from a very important job-getting source. Twenty-five per cent of jobs are found through people's personal contacts, their friends, relations and acquaintances. Whatever your initial feelings, it is totally counter-productive to try and conceal your true situation from others, your family, your friends, relations and neighbours and your business-life contacts or trade acquaintances. There are well-documented cases on record where individuals, usually those who have held more senior positions, have taken this to such an extreme that they have continued the outward manifestations of their working life, leaving the house at the same time in the morning as they used to, and catching the same train up to town as they used to, even though now they have no job to go to. Some, it has been alleged, have been so successful at this concealment of their true situation, that not even wives were aware of their husband's redundancy. Although it is easy with such an extreme case to say that would never happen to you, how sure can you be that you would not try and conceal your redundancy from at least some of your contacts?

It is those contacts who could prove most useful. News of jobs comes in a variety of ways, sometimes from the most unlikely sources. Your task as a job-seeker is to regard getting a job as a full-time occupation and be prepared for this to be as potentially demanding as the job itself. Just as a sales rep can't afford to overlook any sales lead, nor can you afford to overlook any avenue which might lead you to a job. This approach has now become known as 'Networking'.

Regard everyone you know as a potential lead. Let it be known that you are looking for a new job. Not only is it psychologically healthy in that it shows you are facing up to the situation and, more importantly, coping with it – it does actually work. Use especially all the business contacts and trade acquaintances that you've built up over the years. You may well be surprised at the amount of help they can give you. Not only do they have their fingers on the pulse of what is going on within their particular company, they, in a kind of pyramid selling network, can hear of other opportunities outside their own area of operation by talking to their own contacts which would otherwise be closed to you. Once you've overcome the initial hurdle of enlisting their help you will be surprised how useful and generally prepared to help many of them are. Of course there will be one or two who enjoy seeing someone worse off than themselves but the vast majority – especially in today's economic climate – may well be thinking 'There but for fortune . . .' and do their best to help. According to the survey mentioned above, 29 per cent of job-seekers found their new job through trade or professional acquaintances. This is a statistic you can't afford to ignore.

The one final area which you can exploit depends very much on the type of occupation you have had in the past. Many of the trade unions and professional bodies operate a job-finding service for their members. Some don't have the resources to do much more than provide lists of prospective employers, others circulate details of specific opportunities to any of their members who request it, others will offer more of a counselling service which, if you haven't been through the job-seeking exercise before, could be especially useful. If you are a member therefore of any type of organization or professional body it really is well worth exploring what kind of facility they have and what they can offer you. Whatever level of service they provide it will be worthwhile exploiting. It could just lead to the next job.

Planning Your Strategy

This section has dealt with the main ways in which you can find your new job. As we've already mentioned, exploiting these possibilities to their maximum is very much a full-time occupation, especially when you are trying to get the initial momentum going. How best then to plan your strategy of attack? Not all of these approaches can be adopted at once, so it is useful to plan a timetable to try several methods over a set period rather than attempt to achieve it all in a week and then sit back in a combination of boredom and anxiety waiting for developments to occur.

Start by really finding out about the job market, what's on offer, where it's based and what sort of pay is attached. This is done by going through the back issues of the relevant trade press and the national press to see what's on offer, and of course applying for anything recent that is attractive. This will not only give you a good idea of what is available, but will also give an indication of salary levels.

The next stage is to get your CV in front of as many agencies and consultancies as possible and to follow up as recommended earlier in this chapter. There is likely to be a short gap between sending off your CV and getting the response, and this is when you should be scouring the job ads in all the relevant national, local and specialist papers and publications.

Getting the whole process moving is a bit like getting a flywheel started. A tremendous amount of effort is required initially to get the thing moving, but after that effort is put in, the process takes over, requiring only a little (but frequent) input to keep it gathering pace.

Chapter 4

Interviews

All the work you have been putting in to the job search is now paying dividends and you are now receiving invitations to attend interviews. They are likely to fall into three main categories: the general chat; the consultancy interview for a specific job; and the interview with an employer, again for a particular position. What your interviewer is looking for in each of these meetings varies considerably, so we will look at each in some detail.

The General Chat

This usually occurs when a consultancy or company, having received your CV, decide that although they have nothing particularly relevant for you at that moment, they like the look of you on paper and want to see how you check out in real life. It may well be that they have some idea that a suitable position is on the horizon so they think it worthwhile doing a little preliminary investigation. On the other hand if it's an invitation from a headhunter it could be just that they need to get more information on your industry, company, or even of specific individuals within your company, to help them with some other search assignment. If they say they have no suitable job for you but offer to meet you in a club or restaurant, then this, the latter possibility, is probably the case.

Whatever the reason don't pass up the opportunity to go along and see. It is an ideal opportunity to keep in the forefront of their mind's without running the risk of pestering them, and it will provide invaluable experience in the art of being interviewed.

Although they will stress the informality of the session, they will still expect you to be smartly dressed. This is especially true for the middle and senior level appointments. To put it briefly they will be expecting to see H. J. Jones, FCA, Finance Director of XYZ Company and not Harry Jones of Ambleside Villas, devoted husband and father of four just back from the golf club. Dress for the part you wish to project.

The interview itself will most probably be, or appear to be, casual, conversational and unstructured. Be aware however that within this framework your interviewers will be expecting to get some hard information. They will want to have made several value judgements by the end of the interview, concerning your competence, your attitude, your potential to a client company and finally your potential usefulness to them. How they will go about achieving this depends so much on the individual interviewer that it is almost impossible to generalize their approach. We have however listed below in the section on consultancies some of the questions that they are almost certainly bound to ask you, what they are really asking you, and an indication of how best to respond.

To a certain extent, as your interviewers have no precise job in mind, and therefore no detailed job description to relate to your own experience, they will be looking much more at the overall impression. Hence the importance of dressing correctly, the vital importance of attitude, behaviour and 'presence'. Presence is that indefinable air of authority, of being on top of the situation, self-confident without being arrogant, of being inwardly relaxed yet outwardly energetic.

Although this sounds like we are asking you to be everything you least feel like, it is important not to go into an interview emanating nervousness and auras of gloom and despondency brought about by your current situation. These moods are catching and, swapping roles for a moment, would you employ anybody who made you feel anxious and depressed?

They will also be looking for evidence of clear and

positive thinking, articulately expressed. To do this they might well ask you detailed questions about your responsibilities and achievements. Although they will be very interested in what you say, they will be equally interested in how you say it, how well you develop a line of thought, how well you stick to it and how well you express yourself.

One of the most difficult things to assess, especially in a conversational type interview, is simply how much talking you should do. In a normal interview the consultant would not expect to contribute more than 30 per cent of the discussion. In this type of meeting where there is no specific job to discuss, it may well be considerably less. The meeting is after all for them to find out about you. If they try and do more talking than you, then in all probability they are not doing their job properly.

One really has to take each question on its merits. Wide-ranging open questions like 'What were the factors leading up to your redundancy?' deserve detailed, lengthy and considered replies. Coming at the beginning of the interview they are designed to get you talking and to provide individual areas or topics for further questioning and examination. Don't go to either extreme. A terse 'lack of orders' superficially answers the question but all the consultant will do is ask you to expand. On the other hand, although it may be valid to suggest that to answer that particular question fully you need to go back a little, don't whatever you do go right back to the year dot and bore everyone silly with reams of irrelevant history. As in most things it's a question of striking the right balance, and to a limited extent you can take your cue from the interviewer. Watch the body language for signals; if you are interrupted the thought might be that you are embarking on a prepared spiel. On the other hand, if after coming to a pause the response is an encouraging nod you are expected to continue. This can however be a trap, the interviewer hoping that you may say more than you intend to, in an attempt to fill the silence. If in doubt, you won't lose any points by asking outright whether your answer did in fact answer the question, and whether more detail or more expansion of any particular point is required.

It is quite usual at the senior level of the job market for interviewers to ask questions about your company or personnel which, if you are not used to the situation, might sound unnecessarily intrusive and might have you wondering whether you were in danger of breaching any unwritten rules on confidentiality and loyalty to your previous company.

There are two main areas where this may occur – performance figures and the names of individuals within your company. The first is usually a straightforward attempt to assess the company's performance vis à vis your redundancy. Normally the things the interviewers ask you about – turnover, profit before taxation, return on capital – can, in the case of a public company, be gained from the annual report anyway so this need not be regarded as a problem. Asking about these is usually just a means of providing a framework within which your own contribution can be judged. On the other hand, persistent questioning about your colleagues; their strengths and weaknesses and your assessment of their contribution to the company can be viewed at a slightly different level. While the purpose might be simply to find out how you relate with other people, or to assess your attitude regarding working with others, it is perhaps more likely that they are using you to find out more about potential candidates for a different search assignment. How far you go in co-operating with them has to remain a matter for you to decide. Most people are inclined to co-operate in the hope that it will lead to the 'You scratch my back . . .' principle. It certainly won't do any harm as far as that is concerned, but there again, if they rate your abilities and come across a position for which you would be suitable, they won't pass up an opportunity to earn their fee. It's up to you.

Interviews with Consultants: Specific Jobs

Individual consultancies vary tremendously in how much information they will give you about a particular job both before the interview and during it. In many cases you will not know in advance who the client company is. That of course prevents you from doing much of the homework that is essential before meeting a prospective employer. The work you can do prior to the meeting will therefore revolve more around you, your attitudes, abilities and preferences. Don't go to the interview with a 'let's see how it goes' attitude, but think about the type of questions you are likely to be asked. Think positively about the successes in your career to date; work out the information you will need to know from the consultant to make an informed decision about the position and, using whatever you know already about the job – from the original advertisement or a job description they may have sent you – work up a positive enthusiasm for it.

You will probably have heard about the job in one of three ways: through an advertisement; through the consultancy sending you a job specification in response to your sending them a CV; or through them telephoning you, giving you the briefest outline of the envisaged role and inviting you to come in and talk it through. With this last possibility there is little preparation you can do in terms of the job except think things through imagining the role and you in it, what might be expected in terms of the scale of responsibilities, and potential problems to overcome. Perhaps most important of all, think carefully about your skills and experience; select the parts which strike you as being most relevant and be prepared to talk coherently and confidently about them.

If you have anything written at all, such as an ad or job specification, study it carefully. Try and read between the lines. Although they may call the job one thing, do they actually want you to be something a little different? A very common example of this would be a company saying they wanted a marketing manager when what they wanted was someone to take on a sales manager role – their thinking being that marketing sounds higher status than sales. Trying to cut through the in-clichés of the moment, 'young, thrusting, exciting, dynamic, self-starter, future growth potential' etc., can be difficult. Try to work out exactly what the responsibilities are; where the position fits into the structure of the company and then how equipped you are to take on such a role. Once you've done that, work out why: what is it in your experience that suits you for this position? In short try to think things through in as much detail as possible, all the time relating what you know back to your own skills and experience. For it is this connection the consultant is trying to make and it will not go amiss if you can make it easy for him.

The interview itself in terms of style will probably be conducted on very similar lines to the general chat meeting we have just described. It will be conducted in informal surroundings, and more likely around a coffee table than from the other side of the desk. Don't relax too much however because there will be some tight questioning. What we have found as a general rule is that Executive Selection consultants; that is consultants who draw most of their candidates from advertising and from their register, will tell you all about the job at the outset of the interview, ask whether you'd be interested in proceeding and then start asking you questions. Executive Search consultants will however generally launch into their questions straight away and then only if they think you qualify for further consideration will they tell you something about the job to be filled. They will also call the interview a meeting.

Whatever way the consultants decide to conduct the interview, do let them call the tune. It is very tempting to carry on answering one question when they have moved on to a second, especially as you are anxious that full justice is done; that the full circumstances relating to that answer are fully understood. It is also tempting to wrest control of the interview from the consultant, and to fire a barrage of questions back – tempting but not worthwhile. In a sense your role is to win them over so that they act on your behalf in their recommendations to the client. It is of most use to you therefore to be regarded positively, as an ally to help get the assignment completed, rather than someone who is intransigent.

The type of questions you will be asked generally fall into two main areas: that of competence – that you would be able to do the job under offer; and acceptability – that you will fit in to their client structure, and that you will relate well with the personalities within the client company; in short whether you fit the client's image of what they think is needed and, inextricably linked with this, whether the client will like you.

Most of the interview, although apparently talking about the first of these considerations, will in fact be a method of forming an opinion about the second. The CV which you will have provided will, by its career progression, the type of positions held and their attendant responsibilities, plus the length of time in each level, give the consultant quite a lot to work on so far as the question of your competence is concerned. By and large he will be looking for you to validate the claims made in that CV. Remember, consultants will not usually be technically expert in your field, but they are professional recruiters and are usually very quick to spot inflated claims even though they might only have a hazy view, or at least the view of an outsider, of the particular technical method or process you may be describing.

On the other hand, recruitment interviewers are very experienced in deciding what type of person you are and how well you will fit into the particular environment they have in mind. They are quick to detect 'false fronts' and there is no point in pretending to be something you are not. It would be very difficult to sustain through an interview without some kind of anomaly creeping in, let alone through the series of interviews you will probably be asked to attend. More importantly, do you really want a job in which you would have to maintain this pretence? It doesn't work out in the long run.

Be honest but don't hesitate to present matters in their most positive light and in the terms most favourable to you. In addition remember to come across in the most relaxed and self-confident way you can. This is no easy task, but it is what they want to see.

To summarize, the interview with a consultancy is normally an overall examination of your competence through the evaluation of claims you have made either in the CV or during the course of the interview. Far more important than this however is the acceptability factor: is your attitude right, personality right, motivation right, will you please the consultant's client? Overall the most advantageous image to aim for is to be someone who is interested in this particular position because it provides scope for further career progression within the company, and that it's a good company to work for, i.e. it knows how to make best use of its employees. Similarly look at your previous colleagues and employers in an enthusiastic light. Adopt a 'wonderful company, wonderful people, shame it went bust' attitude rather than running everybody down. If you take a very negative attitude, they are more likely to think there is something wrong with you than with your past employer. All the positive things which happened to the company or to you should be presented as a result of individual or team strengths, whereas the negative things were largely brought about by external circumstances.

This is the ideal that most consultants want to hear. They also want it to be true. We are not suggesting in any way that you fabricate or rewrite history but it is useful to know what they are looking for so that you can present your background in the most positive light.

The End of the Interview

Most consultants will allow some time at the end of the meeting to ask whether you have any questions or whether you would like to bring out any points relating to your suitability for the job which perhaps haven't been given full prominence during the discussion. Ask pertinent questions about the client company and the job responsibilities. To get an overall picture, ask about the type of company not only in terms of its balance sheet but also in terms of its philosophy and attitude. Also ask about the personalities of the people who relate to this position. If it's a new post, why was it necessary to create it? If however they are recruiting to replace someone, what happened to the previous encumbent? What are the special priorities and problem areas of the job? You are trying at this stage to establish an overall impression of what it would be like to take the job on, what it would be like to work for the particular company and what scope the job would have for you. Don't try to get into a detailed discussion of very precise specifics or technical minutiae. We are still at too early a stage for this, and to be realistic, it is highly unlikely that the consultant will know the answers anyway.

With the opportunity to promote your own claim to the

job, do make sure that all relevant experience that you have gained has been in fact put forward. The consultant's questioning may have led you away from one or two points that you really should put across to do full justice to yourself. Do keep it brief. Although it can be useful to summarize what you see as the most relevant aspects of your experience compared to the job, again keep it as short, sharp and succinct as possible. Don't give the impression that you're about to run through the whole interview all over again.

At the end the consultants should give you a clear idea of how things should proceed from this stage. Unless you are either very suitable or very unsuitable, the consultants are unlikely to be definite about whether you are through to the next stage. More often than not they won't know, as they firstly will want to reflect on what you've told them, and secondly will still have several more people to see, which may certainly have a bearing on your candidacy. You may well be suitable but they will only be putting forward three or four people in their shortlist. You may still get pipped at the post by those still to come.

They should however give you an indication of when you can expect to hear whether or not they will be taking things further with you. If not, do ask, as there is nothing worse when job seeking than to be left hanging. Should their estimate of the time elapse without your having heard from them, don't hesitate to give them a call. The time span often gets extended through unforeseen circumstances and it won't do any harm to remind them of your existence.

Interviews with Employers

The type of interview you might expect with a company varies tremendously and to such an extent that it is only possible to give a very general overview. Many people who in fact will interview you will be professionally trained or be qualified through experience to conduct such a meeting. On the other hand, on some occasions you will be interviewed by people who have less idea than you about what they should be doing, what questions they should ask and what should have been decided by the end of a session.

By now if you have been shortlisted by a consultancy or, in any case, if you applied direct, you will know the identity of the company. Use the time before the interview as constructively as possible. The areas you should be able to cover are outlined below:

Company Information

Find out as much as you can about the company as possible. If it's a public company then ask them to send you a copy of their annual report. Alternatively use the Extel service in the local reference library to get the company's full financial background. Extel is a card index system containing information on companies such as their financial position and directors' names.

Find out about their products and services. Most companies have brochures which they would be happy to send you. In addition, if their products are accessible, i.e. found on retail shelves, have a good look at them, see how they are packaged and presented, what prominence is given to them and how they are marketed. Although this is peripheral knowledge it can be very useful in assessing their philosophy; how aggressive they are, how marketing-oriented and how confident.

Talk with as many friends, contacts and trade acquaintances as you can. What is their perception of the company? What do they know factually about it, how well is it doing, what kind of reputation does it have as an employer, is it expanding, does it look after its people?

What do you need to know on the technical front? Read up about it.

Job Information

Think the job through as carefully as possible. What are the main responsibilities, and the secondary duties? What will you enjoy doing most/least? What areas of the job have you already done? What will be new? What promotion possibilities exist? How could the existing job develop? How much of a long-term opportunity is it? What problems might you encounter, and how best can you overcome them? What else do you need to know in order to make an informed decision on whether to take the job if offered?

You as Candidate

What strengths in terms of skills and experience can you offer for such a role? What personal qualities are required to fit the role and how do you match up to this? How, in the light of what you know, can you accentuate your strengths and minimize your weaknesses? What technical questions are they likely to ask you, and how well can you answer them? What 'acceptability' questions are they likely to ask? Again, work out your replies.

Improving Your Image

How good are you at being interviewed? A great many people who have found themselves redundant find this is one of the areas where they feel weakest and least prepared. Several of you indeed may find that this is the first real job interview you have had to attend since securing your first job on leaving school. You might have had several internal promotions within the company yet never actually had to apply outside. How will your interview technique compare therefore against those who have moved around? The best advice one can give is that first and foremost you must be yourself. Any kind of put-on act or attempted role play, trying to be what you anticipate the interviewer will want you to be comes across as precisely that. It's not worth the effort.

Having said this, it is possible to sharpen up significantly and improve the overall impression you make. We have mentioned before the need to appear relaxed and confident during the interview. Work on this. Do you have any mannerisms or nervous gestures which might disconcert your interviewer? Most of us do – tugging our ear-lobes, playing with our hair, scratching our nose, playing with cuffs, rings and fingers, and most of us are not aware that we do any of these things. Hold an imaginary interview with your spouse, or friends or relatives. Get them to observe all that you do. Your body language might be transmitting totally different messages to your voice. Of course the ideal way to monitor this is with a video camera. If you own one or can borrow one from a friend, get someone to film you. Then during the playback make a note of all the fiddles and the twiddles you are unconsciously doing. Listen closely to your speech too. (For the sake of this rehearsal rather than imitate a complete interview, just talk through your career to date.) Is it hesitant? Is the substance of what you are saying lost in 'ums' and 'ers'? Does it come across as a continuous narrative or is it disjointed and of spasmodic phrasing? Does every sentence start with 'Well' or 'I think' and so on? Make a list of all the things you didn't like to hear and then try it again, omitting all these faults. You won't succeed in deleting everything, nor do you need to, but you will be surprised at the marked improvement you make. One last point on this. How were you sitting? Were you all hunched up and bending forward? Did you keep moving, shifting your weight continuously, crossing and uncrossing your legs? Were you on the other hand leaning back so far, or sitting at such an angle it looked like you might cant gently back off the chair? Again notice what you were doing, the impression it made and how you can improve on it.

Obviously it is not always easy to get hold of a video camera, but it will help you immensely if you can. If you can't get hold of one then try and go through the interview with a friend, with another person acting as an impartial observer. You can certainly learn a lot this way and it was in fact the method used on most training courses before use of the video camera became so widespread.

You can of course get professional help. The career counselling concerns which we will be discussing in the next chapter will certainly offer services in this respect, but you will have to pay for it. Why not however try to get assistance from the personnel department of the company you are leaving? They will almost certainly be experienced in the art of recruitment interviewing and most probably very pleased to give you whatever assistance they can. Of course they are likely to be more responsive if you are still with the company, so try and get your request in early rather than at the last minute.

To meet the growing demand for advice, some of the major selection and search firms offer free evening 'Job Hunting workshops' for senior managers; the London office of Price Waterhouse being one which springs to mind. This is very professionally run and can give useful insights into CV presentation and interview techniques, as well as other aspects of job hunting. It is well worthwhile attending such a course.

Final Preparations

Having prepared yourself mentally for the interview, there are the obvious practical tasks to get sorted out. What are you going to wear? Is it clean, pressed and smart looking, and are your shoes in good shape? How are you travelling? By car, bus, train? Find out the times and make sure you leave in good time. Do you know exactly how to find the building? If not, check it out, phone their switchboard and get specific directions. If travelling by car, leave in plenty of time, adding on time for hold-ups, breakdowns etc., and check everything over before you leave to minimize the risk. Finally what do you need to take with you? The spare CV? The job information, references, proof of qualifications, certificates of technical competence? Your portfolio of work? Examples of articles you have written? Depending on what your job is and what you are applying for, you might find all, none or some of these are necessary. The important thing is to think it through well in advance so there is no last-minute panic.

Arrival

Try and get to the place of interview a little before the time indicated. Make sure you are never late. No matter how junior or senior the job, punctuality will be regarded as being of great importance. In making sure you are not late, if you find you are much too early it is preferable to find a coffee bar in the locality and while away the time there rather than arriving too early. Arriving at 2.30 for a 3.30 meeting doesn't mean you'll be seen any earlier. Your interviewers will no doubt be on a very tight time schedule and won't be able to alter it to accommodate you. At best they won't be aware of your presence until your allotted time and at worst you will be a constant niggle at the back of their minds while they try to concentrate on other matters. It's not conducive to getting the interview off to a good, friendly and positive start. The optimum time to arrive is 5 to 10 minutes before the scheduled start. This gives you time to make the necessary enquiries at reception, be escorted to the appropriate part of the building and to settle down and compose yourself before the interview proper.

Normally you shouldn't have to wait more than 5 or 10 minutes but things often go wrong, even in the best regulated of companies. Do therefore take something to read and try not to get too steamed up about the delay. The interviewers will often pass through reception before introducing themselves to you so it would be better if they didn't catch you stormily pacing up and down or demanding of the receptionist what the hell is going on. There is no need to assume that delays are aimed at you personally. They are more likely to be due to late arrival of previous candidates, but some people do seem to keep you waiting deliberately either as a method of 'psyching' you up or to try and prove how busy and important they are. It is an arrant display of rudeness, but you do yourself no favours at all by letting it get to you. Go back to whatever you are reading and if the receptionist offers you coffee, accept it but try not to smoke – it might be taken as proof that you need an external prop to cope – and comfort yourself with the thought that you've seen through their performance and it doesn't upset you and you are therefore one up on them.

If you have not already done so, you may be asked to complete a standard application form when you arrive. This is where the spare CV is useful for reminding you of all those bits of information which disappear from your mind just when you want them such as starting and finishing dates of jobs, and examination grades. Often this period is used to settle your expenses. If either a company or consultancy invite you to discuss a specific vacancy, then they should and normally will offer you expenses. How much to claim? The golden rule is not to try and use this as a way of augmenting your income, no matter how needy you are. Claim only what is reasonable and that is what you have actually incurred. Especially in today's straitened times expenses claims do get examined and, no matter how suitable you may be for a particular job, you won't get offered it if the company thinks you're already trying to exploit them.

Claiming Expenses

What to do if the company doesn't volunteer to pay expenses is often a source of considerable embarrassment to candidates. Will asking for them create the wrong impression? If it is a reputable company it certainly shouldn't. It is a very well-established convention that the company pays candidates' expenses and should it not be mentioned it is normally due more to administrative oversight than deliberate evasion. When however to ask? During the closing stages of the interview you will often be asked if there is anything else you want to cover in respect of the job. Don't however mix up an expenses claim with discussion of the job. Wait till everything is over and you are now quite sure that the offer (for expenses) isn't coming from them as you are shown towards the door, ask whether you should see the interviewer's secretary on the way out to put in for your expenses. Handled like this no one can take offence; it is kept separate from the job interview itself and you won't miss out. Alternatively, write to them once you are back home re-stating your commitment to the position and enclosing a note itemizing expenses incurred.

The Interviews

The interviews themselves can be as varied as the people who will be conducting them. Apart from seeing a person from the personnel department, the main interviewer is most likely to be a senior member of the function or department you will be working within or it may be the person you will actually report to within that function should you take the job. You might well see the head of the department after a full interview with the first manager.

If you are applying for a senior position you may well miss seeing the personnel function altogether and go straight to the appropriate board director and/or chief executive.

At any level most companies will operate a checking system in that the decision whether to employ you is confirmed by a more senior member of the company. You can expect therefore to be interviewed by more than one person although this needn't necessarily be on the same day. Also, perhaps mainly for internal communications and politics, they may decide that quite a number of people within the company should have the power to approve or veto any appointment. You are therefore shown through a bewildering number of offices with brief almost cursory and identical questioning from each. Not only do you have to bear with this; you also have to use it positively. What sort of people are they? Could you work with them? Indeed would you enjoy doing so?

The thing to do is to take each type of interview on its merits to take things as they come and to try to enjoy each experience as much as possible without of course forgetting your prime purpose; that is, to get the job!

The Interview with the Personnel Department

This will normally be geared very much to two main subjects. They will be looking at you in very much the same way as a consultant in order to assess your 'acceptability factor'; whether, in terms of attitude, personality, motivation and interpersonal skills, you fit into the structure of the company, and whether you are likely to be able to work with existing colleagues. They will almost certainly ask you about your work, what you do and to try and establish how well you do it, but this, even more than the consultancy interview will be geared to finding out about you as a person rather than your technical competence. After all, following your meeting with personnel you will be interviewed by line management who will be much more able and much better equipped to talk to you about the technical content of the job and your achievements in this respect.

The other part of the interview will be a much more factual information-giving session mainly linked to your welfare should you join the company. It is likely to include details of their pension arrangements, sick and holiday pay, significant benefit, performance related incentives, free travel, car, free or subsidized meals and relocation assistance. They will often too give you details of their appraisal and review systems – how you will be assessed in your job plus an outline of potential promotion paths and prospects.

The Interview with the Line Manager

Getting this right is probably the single most important stage in the whole process of job search for this is the person you will report to if and when you join the company. Personnel managers will usually present a shortlist of vetted candidates and senior managers will reserve the right to veto any particular applicant, but the line manager will make the largest part of the decision about whether to employ you. This is the important one therefore and it is perhaps ironically the case that very often this is the person who has least experience in interviewing skills and practice. Don't be dismayed by this, use it positively and to your advantage.

The primary concern will be to establish your ability to do the job needing to be filled. Although no doubt you will be asked once again to go through your background and skills acquired, you are much more likely to have thrown at you hypothetical situations and to be asked how you would cope. Take each of these on its merits. You can be pretty sure that although they are presented to you as being hypothetical, they are in fact real examples of either recent or current problems. This, apart from giving you useful insight into the way the operation is currently run, gives you a glimpse of the problems you are likely to face if you accept the position.

Don't just give the first answer that comes into your head. Make sure you have all the information you need to reach a sensible decision. If not, ask for further details on the hypothesis until you feel equipped to make a recommendation. Say also what you believe to be true rather than what you think the person wants to hear. Everybody likes to be agreed with, but trying to follow that line in this type of situation can make things more difficult. People will, in general, react more favourably to an opposing view cogently expressed than to a 'me too, I agree' type answer which hints of sycophancy. Always however keep the answer firmly in the realms of hypothesis and always acknowledge that there are alternative ways of solving the problem.

In this way you can avoid conflict but still get evidence of your original thinking across. The last thing you want is to get into a confrontation with your prospective boss. If it looks like developing into this – after all, you might just have unwittingly contradicted a pet scheme, do be prepared to back down gracefully. After all, the boss will be looking to appoint someone to work with and not feel threatened by. Human nature being what it is you can be fairly sure that should you win the argument you might lose the job. Although you will hear frequent trumpetings to the contrary, nobody likes appointing someone beneath them who is clearly brighter than themselves.

Do try and build up a rapport with this person. Although the stated aim might be to assess your technical suitability, it is reasonable to assume that you will be in competition with similarly qualified people for the post. In the final analysis, who they offer the job to will be decided largely by who they feel they can work with best. Be appreciative of what they have to tell you therefore and be impressed by at least certain aspects of their existing operation.

The Interview with Senior Managers: The Corroborative Interview

Getting this far means that you're doing well. Often before a line manager makes a final decision you will be passed up to his manager or board director for him to have a look at you. They will be relying heavily on the recommendations made from lower down in terms of their assessment of your competence so this will be a meeting heavily weighted to assess your acceptability. Try not to be overawed. Use all the skills you have been practising and developing in terms of appearing relaxed and confident and, above all, highly motivated and keen. Don't be inhibited in suggesting new ideas. This person, being one stage removed, will feel less threatened by them and will appreciate hearing evidence of your ability to make an innovative contribution to the company.

Often this meeting will be conducted in a fairly free and informal atmosphere. Indeed if you're going for a more senior job this meeting may well be over drinks or lunch. As a general rule, if in doubt about the social etiquette, just take your lead from your hosts. Drink marginally less and slightly more slowly than they do. You don't want them to think that by not drinking you are puritanically disapproving, but there again drinking more than they do runs the risk of being labelled a lush. Similarly with food, don't choose anything awkward to eat, try and establish what they are ordering and choose something comparable in price and type. If they throw the decision on to you to order, steer down the middle course in terms of price and don't try and impress in your knowledge of wines unless you are very sure of your ground. Again go for the middle price range and where possible throw the decision back at them by asking what they would prefer. Moderation has to be the way; don't give them any kind of hook on which to hang an objection to you.

The Interview: General Points

Don't go into the interview negatively thinking that your interviewers will be determined to trip you up or catch you out. Remember they are just as anxious to get the job filled as you are to fill it. But they do want to get the best possible person for the job so they will try and stretch you a little to see how capable you are. Regard this positively; see it as a challenge.

Sometimes they will be as inexperienced as you in the interview situation and there are always ways to take advantage of this. Gently take control by asking questions about the job. This shows enthusiasm and while they are answering they are not probing your areas of potential weakness.

Remain cool, whatever the situation. They might be abrupt or too busy to take the interview as seriously as they should. If, for example, you are being interviewed by someone whose phone is constantly ringing and subject to all sorts of interruptions and distractions, don't get rattled. Just acknowledge privately to yourself that this is a potential winning situation for you because this person clearly doesn't know what he's doing and can't concentrate fully on you.

We have described several typical interview situations which cover the majority of interviews you are likely to face. Each company has its own pet ways of doing things so always be alert to different situations. Some might handle it by grouping several managers together to interview you, some might even put you into a competitive situation. Take each on its merits, remain outwardly cool, relaxed and confident, and take things as they come. It is a truism that the interview is won or lost in the first five minutes and the remainder of the time used to justify that original impression. It's not as simple as that, as we hope this chapter makes clear, but if you start off relaxed and confident you are half-way to success.

Key Questions

There is no way to predict with absolute certainty what questions you will be asked. This list however gives some of the most common questions which are designed to assess your acceptability rather than your technical competence, together with an indication of how best to respond.

1. What were the factors leading up to your redundancy?
i.e. Is your redundancy genuine or is it a euphemism for dismissal? As we have previously mentioned, you should give a full answer emphasizing if at all possible that it was external circumstances which led to the situation. It will however lead into question 2.

2. What steps, with the benefit of hindsight, could have been taken which might have prevented your redundancy?
This is obviously more of a danger to senior executives rather than those lower down the organization chart who

have had less say (if any) in the decisions which led to the redundancy situation. For the most senior levels, be very alert to this question as it really is designed to dig into your attitudes as well as questioning your capacity to hold a senior job. If for example you try to suggest that it was completely inevitable then their reaction is most likely to put you down as a pessimistic fatalist, lacking foresight, initiative and drive.

If on the other hand it was everybody else's fault but your own, you are equally certain to lose credibility. Similarly if you are too wise with hindsight then doubts are cast on your foresight. Not many interviewers would resist asking, 'Well, if you can see all that now why couldn't you see it then?'

At the other extreme if you claim that no one could have foreseen what in fact occurred then again your foresight and forward planning abilities get marked down.

The best answer is to be as honest as possible and take time to outline each step in the chain, what happened, why it happened, what remedies you suggested, why they failed/were successful at that stage. If asked why, if you could see problems, you didn't try and get out sooner, do counter that by mentioning your loyalty to the company.

3. Why are you interested in this position?
This is sometimes a difficult one purely because at the stage it is asked you haven't been given a full picture of what is involved. If you have an ad or job specification to work on pick out various areas which sound either interesting or challenging and then tell them so and why. Explain how it fits into your ideas for your planned career progression from this point. Never ever use the 'Gi's a job' approach or 'I just want a job' or that 'the money looked good'. These might be precisely the reasons why you have applied but it always upsets employers and consultants alike. They always want you to be highly motivated and enthusiastic about 'their' job. If you're just interested in any job then their inclination is to leave you alone so you can go off and find 'just any job'.

4. Where do you hope to be in five to ten years' time?
Most people have long-range goals and this is designed

to uncover them. What they are really asking is how ambitious you are and also how realistic. Although you might feel that all you want to think about is getting a job now, it is worth thinking this one through as it will help you decide whether the job in question does in fact fit in with your plan. To use an analogy, when attempting to solve those printed puzzles of mazes where you have to work out which entrance out of several choices leads to the middle, it is easier to start at the middle and work outwards. Similarly it sometimes can be a help in career terms to work out where you want to end up and then plot your course back accordingly step by step. To answer this question, however, a flexible approach is probably the best. It is particularly useful as it can be used to bring out certain facets of your skills and experience which otherwise might not get the mention they deserve. An example could be 'If I built on the marketing experience I have gained then . . . on the other hand I have got a lot out of my experience running the finance department in the subsidiary company. Of course, ideally I would aim eventually for a role which called on both areas and which would be that of General Manager of a small- to medium-sized company in engineering products' – or whatever. Make sure however that one of your possible scenarios is directly linked to taking the job under discussion as a first step or at least something closely akin to it. Otherwise the net result might be to leave the interviewer wondering what on earth you're doing there.

5. What would you describe as being your main strengths and weaknesses?

These plus and minus questions always get asked and are always difficult to answer. It is essential, as part of your homework, to have really thought them through. They fall into two main types. The first includes those which relate ostensibly to the job. What were the most satisfying/dissatisfying aspects of your last job? What were you able to do in which you felt you were particularly effective/ineffective? What do you feel you accomplished which was most/least successful etc. Although you will be relating your answer to aspects of the job which certainly will interest the interviewer, he or she will also be listening very carefully to what you are saying in terms of yourself, your attitudes and your blind spots.

This is even more pronounced when you are asked a question which comes out of the second type: a bald enquiry about you, your strengths and weaknesses, how effective/ineffective you are; what you regard as your positives and negatives, and so on. Most of the pluses are self-evident but be prepared to justify them in terms of specific examples. Where possible pick them so they have some relationship with what is required in the job under discussion.

The negatives are a much more difficult matter. Everybody has relative weaknesses so you can't avoid the issue by answering 'none'. Whatever you do, don't assume the role of patient on a psychiatrist's couch and startle everyone, yourself included, by unleashing a torrent of self-doubt. It is one of the few areas in the interview where being totally frank isn't really in your best interests. You are quite justified in regarding it as being the interviewer's job to find these out, and therefore not handing them over on a plate. Having said that however it will help you tremendously if you appear to give a constructive and reasoned answer. Stress that you think they are weaknesses only in relative terms to your strengths. Perhaps then pile on one or two of the strengths which seemed to go down well and then add 'too'. For example 'Perhaps in a particular set of circumstances I was too . . . ambitious, determined, conscientious' or whatever. Do remember however that weaknesses in one situation can be regarded as strengths if placed in a different context, and work from there. Finally don't be afraid to admit to mistakes you've made in the past – not too many, but some. Everybody makes them and if you deny that you ever have, you will lose credibility.

6. How do you get on with the people you work with? Basically a question to get your views on people-management, how you liaise with colleagues in other functions, how well you take orders and how well you motivate your team, how much of a leader and how much of a team player you are. It's really to find out whether your style will fit in with others in the company, or if applicable, with customers and clients. In some jobs, line-management will be of great significance and, if applying for such a job, be prepared to be questioned closely on the subject. Otherwise it is, as we say, merely a way of assessing how well you will fit in. Give a reasoned reply stressing how you like to gain the co-operation of others but know when you have to make a 'stand', and, although you might be asked to give instances, that will usually suffice.

Note: We have concentrated in this chapter principally on how to handle interviews as this is still by far the most preferred method of recruitment. Other forms and methods of selection are however growing in popularity. Psychometric testing, once a rarity, is now commonplace. The tests used vary considerably but fall into two main groups. The first is aptitude or ability tests which are given under controlled conditions and within a set time limit. These test a wide range of skills but the most commonly used will be either to assess your numerical or, alternatively, your verbal reasoning skills. If you are in a specialized occupation such as engineering or design you might come across tests designed to assess your spatial skills or your ability to solve problems in a three-dimensional context. Obviously with all these tests the assessor is looking at your ability to arrive at the right answers under strict time limits.

On the other hand there are personality questionnaires which strictly speaking shouldn't be called tests at all as there are no right or wrong answers. These ask you to give your preferences; either by getting you to choose between options or, alternatively, by agreeing or disagreeing with given statements. Usually no time limit is given within which to complete the questionnaire, although it is generally better to work through it as quickly as possible, giving the answers which first come to mind rather than agonize over or attempt to second guess which answer is preferred. There are no right or wrong answers and the questionnaires are designed to reveal how you go about your work, your relationships with other people and your emotional state.

Usually tests or questionnaires will be used to augment

the information gleaned from the interview rather than be a 'make or break' in themselves. If you are asked to do these tests, try and be as truthful as possible, and always ask for feedback on how well you've done. This is helpful to focus your job hunting if any further is needed.

Chapter 5

How to Cope: Mind and Body

The previous chapters have concentrated mainly on the practical implications of redundancy and how to cope with them. However, redundancy is a problem which can affect not only our financial and employment statuses, but also our physical and mental health. Different people react to redundancy in different ways, not only because of personality differences between different people, but also because of the circumstances surrounding redundancy. The four classical stages of reactions to redundancy were outlined in the introduction but they will now be gone into in more depth.

Stage 1: Shock

Just how much redundancy comes as a shock will be determined by the circumstances surrounding your individual redundancy and also by whether you have ever been made redundant before. If this is your first redundancy you will be much more worried about the situation than you will if you have already experienced redundancy and know you can survive. The extent of the shock will also depend on how you find out about your redundancy. If redundancy has been in the air for some months and the whole company or department is involved, then the announcement may even come as a relief. The tension is over and at least you know where you are. If only a proportion of the workforce is to be made redundant, you may however have been hoping that you would not be selected and the news that you are one of the unlucky few can be a bitter blow. Although most people will have some idea that redundancy was on the cards, the news can sometimes come completely out of the blue:

> *It was ten to five and I was called into the Managing Director's office. My manager was sitting there and I could see that something was wrong, but I had no idea what. Then the Managing Director held out an envelope and said, 'I'm terribly sorry but we are having to make you redundant. As you know business is not very good at present and we are having to make cutbacks. I would like to take this opportunity of thanking you for all you have done for us.' The envelope contained a month's money; I had been with the company only a year and ten months and wasn't entitled to any redundancy money. The Managing Director said I could finish work today and come back and clear my desk tomorrow. I looked at my manager hoping he would say something, but he just looked embarrassed. I went back to the office and it was obvious from the looks on the other girls' faces that they had known all day. I was so stunned I just couldn't do anything. I wanted to cry but I couldn't even do that. I just took my handbag and coat and ran out of the office.*
>
> Former Sales Order Clerk, aged 25

For this woman redundancy had come as a complete shock. There were often peaks and troughs in the orders, but there was plenty of filing and other things which she could catch up on when business was slack and she had been busily working up until the moment she was called into the Managing Director's office. It had not occurred to her that her job would cease to exist. For others however redundancy has been looming on the horizon for some time.

> *The lay-offs started two years ago. First it was just the young lads and lasses, the ones who couldn't claim any redundancy. First it was the sales girls; to tell you the truth they had always been a bit over-staffed, but they cut them right back, so in the end they were trying to watch two or*

three counters at a time. And what with the pressure of trying to serve everybody and the supervisors on their backs all the time to stop the thieving, some of the school kids and these unmarried mums around here are terrors, some of them just left anyway. But what with all the redundancies in the factories, nothing was selling and they needed fewer and fewer men in the warehouse unloading and what have you. So first, as I said, they got rid of the young lads and my mates said, 'We'll be all right, it'll be last-in-first-out, all the way along the line. We'll be the last to go.' But, of course, you can't have a warehouse with all the labour over 50. You need the youngsters to do the really heavy work. So they made all us over-50s redundant. My mates were surprised but I wasn't. I'd seen it coming all along. I was glad to get out really. It's heavy work for a man my age.

Former Warehouseman, retail store, aged 52

The first time I was made redundant it was a shock. That was back in the seventies when redundancy was only starting to affect executives. None of my friends or neighbours had ever been unemployed, except perhaps in the gap between leaving university and getting a first job, and people didn't know how to take it. This time it was much better. I knew the company was in a bad way and they would either have to lose staff or go under. Most of the other managers had been there a lot longer than me, so if anyone was going to be picked out, I was the obvious choice. Fortunately, having been made redundant once, I knew the signs, so I had been putting out feelers for some time. By the time they actually told me, I had more or less fixed myself up with another job. I didn't tell them that immediately though. I negotiated a good deal with them and let them know later I had another job to go to. I thought they might be less generous if they thought I wasn't going to be unemployed.

Production Manager, aged 42

Redundancy need not necessarily be a shock and employers should endeavour to make sure that it isn't. Many managements are reluctant to let their workers have any inkling that there may be redundancies in case it starts a mass exodus to other jobs. As soon as companies are

103

certain that redundancies will have to be made, however, the workforce should be informed. Redundancy should never be sprung on anyone.

Some people, whilst expecting redundancies to happen, will not expect them to happen to them. If redundancy is on a departmental basis or the last-in-first-out formula, then it will be easy for employers to explain why someone has been selected and from the employee's point of view, he or she need not feel that the redundancy is a reflection on them. But supposing redundancy is not made on some arbitrary criterion, but on grounds of performance, and you have been selected because your performance is poor. Your first reaction may be not only shock, but despair. Success is highly prized in Western society and when we do not succeed, there are few safety nets. If this is your situation you are going to have to take a very firm hold of yourself. What is going to be most important is not what is past, but how you come to terms with and overcome the present situation. You must judge yourself on your success or failure in coping with the present crisis, not on what you have failed to do in the past.

What you must do is to accept the situation and analyse why you were not a success in your job. You must firstly decide if yours was an absolute failure or a relative failure. If you were selected for redundancy because your company is amalgamating its sales areas and your performance was worse than your rival's in the adjoining area, this does not necessarily mean you were a poor sales representative. You may have made your target every month and have been one of the best sales representatives in the company. However you could still have been made redundant if the representative in the area with which yours is being amalgamated made double the target. If your sales skills are not Olympic standard, they may still be European championship standard and you could well be another firm's best sales rep. So in making an objective assessment of your performance, you will have to take account of the competition. This type of situation is, of course, one where you should have a very careful discussion with your employer about the wording of references. There is a world of difference between, 'We had to make John redundant because he was the worse salesman,' and 'Although John was one of our best salesmen and has consistently made target every month in the three years he has been with us, we have had to make him redundant.'

If yours is a relative failure then you will have suffered a setback but you can come back on the rebound. What if you were just plain bad at the job? It is helpful here to be very honest with yourself and to sit down with a piece of paper and a pen and write down what went wrong. Make two columns and head them 'Reasons' and 'Solutions'. Below are some 'Reasons' why your performance may have been poor and some solutions to the problems.

Reasons	*Solution*
Poor health of self or family member	Return to same kind of work after recovery; or, if health not improving, return to less demanding work, considering early retirement if applicable
Dislike of job content	Change to a different job or retrain
Dislike of company/boss, workmates etc.	Change to a different company
Over-promoted	Take a job a step down
Poor management skills	Take a job which does not require supervision of others
Poor technical skills	Attend training course or change job
Under-employed	Look for a better job, obtain training which will allow you to get a better job

Unless your performance has declined because of unforeseen factors such as illness, you are not solely to blame if you have done badly in your job. Your employer's judgement in hiring you was also at fault. Your employer should do all he or she can to help you get into the right type of job. Ask your employer why you were not good at the job and what sort of job he or she thinks you could be good at. If you have been employed at management level, the company may if you ask be willing to pay for the services of professional careers counsellors to help you make an objective analysis of where your talents do lie. This is discussed further in Chapter 6.

However your redundancy has come about, whether in ways which do not threaten your self-esteem or ways which do, to get yourself over the initial shock you must act and start thinking about how you are going to cope.

Stage 2: Optimism

Once you start doing something about the situation, you will find yourself in the optimistic stage of redundancy. Some people, such as the production manager quoted above, manage to avoid the shock stage altogether. You are likely to remain in the optimism stage as long as you can maintain your positive and active approach to your situation. In Chapter 1 we mentioned 'locus of control'. Those who have an internal locus of control feel that they are in control of events and those with an external locus of control feel that events are in control of them. If you start sitting back waiting for things to happen to you, you will rapidly start thinking like a victim and depression will set in. Instead you must take charge of yourself and your situation and decide how you are going to manage it. The first essential is to decide how you are going to organize your working day. We use the term 'working day' deliberately, because job hunting is in itself a job and will be, from now until you are back in employment, your full-time occupation.

To maintain your optimism your working day needs to be fully occupied. You must not sink into 'unemployed' habits and start getting up in the middle of the day. This will save on the heating bills, but at the expense of making you introverted and depressed. Instead get up at your usual time and spend the time that you would previously have spent fighting your way into the train or sitting nose to tail in the early morning traffic jam around the industrial estate on some form of healthy exercise. Now is the golden opportunity to take up the daily jogging or swimming you always promised yourself when you were working, but never quite had time for. Alternatively you could do a dance work-out or simply walk the dog. Vigorous exercise has the plus point of releasing brain chemicals called endorphins into your bloodstream. Endorphins raise your pain threshold, protect you against stress and make you feel generally glad to be alive. As you jog round the park listening to the birds, allow yourself to muse for a moment on the joys of a temporary release from the treadmill of work before you begin the serious business of getting back on that treadmill. When you go back to work you want to go back both physically and mentally fitter than when you left. Hopefully leaner, lighter, with a healthy glow and knowing a lot more about yourself.

As well as your exercise habits, you should take this opportunity to overhaul your eating habits. Most people's food budgets include all sorts of items which are not only expensive and unnecessary, but positively unhealthy. Because of pressures in your working life you might have had time only to grab junk food and 'eat on the run' rather than eat properly. For a healthy diet you need a good balance of protein, carbohydrates, fats, fibres, vitamins and minerals. Ideas about diet have changed radically in the last few years. Red meat and animal fat are now frowned on, as are excessive dairy products. For protein choose white meat, fish, nuts and beans in preference to red meats. They are not only healthier but in most cases cheaper. Get your carbohydrates from wholemeal bread and other wholemeal flour products. Eat fresh salad and vegetables rather than high-priced and over-processed frozen vegetables whose vitamin content has been destroyed. If you feel you need more guidance about what you should be eating, visit your local library or health food shop and read up on the subject. The saying 'You are what you eat' is literally true, so make sure you are eating the right things. When you come back from your exercise have a healthy breakfast – wholemeal toast, muesli, etc., not a bacon fry-up. Now is the chance to get fit and healthy.

You are now ready for the day ahead. Your days must be carefully planned so you use your time in the most productive way. You will have to work your schedule around interviews and signing-on days, so it will vary from week to week. Spend at least part of every day out of the house. If you spend all day within your own four walls, you will become lethargic and bored. The less you do the less you will feel like doing, so make sure you plan your days to be useful and active.

Exactly how you plan your week will depend on your own individual circumstances, but the table on page 109 gives you an idea of what you should aim towards. First, note that we recommend that you devote one major part of each day to job seeking. Second, go out every day. This saves on heating bills at home and acts against losing contact with the outside world. Many unemployed people make the mistake of going out less and less, until it becomes an effort to go out at all. Third, get some form of physical exercise which will make you feel better in mind and body and will also make you sleep better. Fourth, be well-organized. Plan ahead for job interviews and make sure you are well-briefed.

Note, too, that our job-seeker is not such a model of Puritan virtue that no time is allowed to take advantage of any of the cheap daytime concessions unemployed status affords. Take advantage of the cheap rate offered at the local authority's squash courts to keep up your game. If you are wondering who you will get to play squash with you in the afternoons, then put a notice on the club noticeboard along the lines of:

'Temporarily displaced executive seeks partner to take advantage of cheap afternoon squash rates'

and you should soon find someone.

This brings up another point. Many unemployed people instinctively prefer to avoid others who are unemployed. This is not a particularly good idea. If you have no unemployed friends, you can start to feel a bit of a freak and forget that there are millions of others just like you. It is useful to have at least one unemployed friend with whom you can discuss your feelings and problems which are particularly derived from your unemployment. Whilst your employed friends can be sympathetic, unless they have been unemployed themselves, they cannot share the experience. You will also find it reassuring that other unemployed people have much the same feelings as you

Day	MORNING		AFTERNOON		EVENING	
Mon.	Visit temporary job agencies. Has anyone failed to turn up for a booking?	Visit library, scan job ads and read newspapers. Copy out any relevant job ads.	Write application letters. If no relevant ads have appeared write some speculative letters to companies.		Check interview suit for Wednesday.	Attend evening class in French.
Tues.	Put suit in cleaners.	Visit library to check newspapers and do some company research for Wednesday's interview.	Mug up on company research, read Wednesday's job spec., work out questions likely to be asked.	Visit Job Centre. Collect suit. Visit station to check train times for tomorrow.	Check everything is ready for tomorrow.	Do the family accounts.
Weds.	Job Interview.		Go home and change out of interview suit. Make notes on interview. What questions did you answer well, badly. What should you remember next time?	Visit library to check job ads, read newspapers and write applications.	Voluntary work teaching on Adult Literacy Scheme.	
Thurs.	Visit library to read job ads.	Sign on.	Play squash.		Attend evening class on Public Speaking.	
Fri.	Visit Job Centre. Arrange interview for a telephone order clerk vacancy for Monday.	Visit temp agencies.	Visit library to check ads, write applications if there are any suitable jobs. Do company research for Monday's interview.		Work on allotment.	

Vertical dividers between the paired columns: **BREAKFAST AND EXERCISE** (morning), **LUNCH** (afternoon), **DINNER** (evening).

Typical Job Hunter's Week

do. If you don't have a friend who is unemployed you may find one through an ad such as the one above. Some people find it beneficial to team up with someone else who is unemployed and to do their job hunting together. Visits to the library will be more fun if you know there is going to be a friendly face there and there is someone to eat a sandwich with later. You can also keep your eyes and ears open for jobs for one another. If a few of you are made redundant from the same office or work, you may want to team up with a friend from work. It is not however a good idea to team up with someone who does exactly the same job as you. When jobs are scarce, job rivalry can put a strain on any friendship and you do not want to be competing for exactly the same vacancies.

On a more formal basis job clubs have been set up by the employment agencies which actively embody these principles. One does, however, have to be unemployed for a period of not less than 6 months before being eligible for these, so it is a good idea to get your own ad-hoc version going immediately if at all possible.

You will see from the timetable that our job-seeker is brushing up on various skills. This is something you may have felt disinclined to do when your time and attention were absorbed by work. Now you have more excess energy, it is wise to bring up to date any skills you may have. A knowledge of French, word processors, or the latest production technique may make a crucial difference to your job chances. Many people receive their professional journals and file them away without ever really reading them. Dig these out and find out what is going on in your job or industry. If you are a secretary and your shorthand is rusty, take advantage of local authority evening classes to bring it up to scratch. If you know you are inarticulate at interviews, join a discussion or public speaking class and do something about the problem. Learning new skills and developing old ones builds up our confidence in ourselves. When we feel competent, we also feel confident, and confidence is essential to keep us in the optimistic stage of redundancy.

If you have worked your way up from the shop-floor and now find yourself competing with people with qualifications, then do not sit back and bemoan the fact that you haven't got any. Get yourself registered with either a part-time class or a correspondence course and get yourself some. Many Institutes require you to be working in the profession in order to register as a student member, so get this done before you leave your employer. Improving your qualifications is another area where your employer may be willing to help out. If you think lack of formal qualifications is likely to be a handicap in getting another job, ask your employer if he would be willing to pay your tuition fees for a correspondence or other course. Even if you are not qualified, if you can put on your CV that you are a student member of the Institute and are studying for qualifications, this shows that you are trying and that you have a genuine interest in your professional development.

If your literacy is poor, you will not be reading this book, but if you are a friend or relative of a redundant person who does not have good reading and writing skills, then ensure that they do something about it. Anyone who cannot successfully complete an application form will find it very hard to get a job in today's increasingly paper-dominated world. Even if you are going for a very unskilled labouring job, you will be asked to fill in a simple form giving details of your past work experience and this can be a nightmare to anyone with poor literacy. Your local authority education department will be able to give you details of the Adult Literacy Scheme and your local jobcentre or TEC will be able to tell you about the Employment Training 'Preparatory' courses which are designed to improve the educational standard of those seeking jobs and/or training.

The Adult Literacy Scheme brings us to the final point to be made about our job-seeker's timetable – voluntary work. When you are redundant and unemployed it is very easy to feel that you are on the receiving end of what other people choose to dole out to you. For your own sense of self-esteem and self-respect, you do not want to feel that you are permanently taking from others and giving nothing back. Going out and doing something for other people is one of the best ways of reminding yourself that you are not a social parasite and that you have something you can give others, and also of turning your attention away from your own problems and getting them into perspective. If these do not seem particularly altruistic motives for helping others, don't worry, they don't have to be. People do things for other people because they enjoy it and benefit from it and it should be a two-way thing. Different types of voluntary work are discussed further in Chapter 8, together with ways of improving your skills through training and education.

This timetable does not allow any time for housework, cooking and shopping. If you have been in the habit of doing household chores when you were working, then fit them in around your day in much the same way as you did before. If you did the housework when you came in for the evening, then continue to do so. It is very tempting to start devoting more and more of your day to unnecessary household activity. If you are a D.I.Y. fanatic, redundancy can seem the ideal opportunity to catch up on all those jobs which you have been meaning to do for years, but however much satisfaction you get from your lovely built-in wardrobe, there will be little point in having it if you cannot afford the clothes to put in it. By all means allow yourself to spend a bit more time on these activities than you would when you are working, but they must not become your major daily activity – that must be job hunting.

If you have not previously done any of the household chores and your partner is not working, they will not feel that you should be taking on some of the burden if you are out and about looking for jobs. If you stay at home all day it could be a very different story. When wives and husbands are suddenly forced to spend every waking moment together this can put a great strain on marriage. You will both be much happier if you go out and allow your partner to carry on as normal. Remember also that Parkinson's Law operates as far as household activities are concerned; they expand to fill the time available. You may when you were working have had to do your shopping in the Friday evening late-night crush. Obviously if you can now shop at less crowded times of the day, there is no point in not doing so, but be careful that shopping does not become a daily activity gradually expanding to fill whole mornings at a time. If you were in the habit of shopping once a week, continue to shop once a week, but choose a less crowded time, preferably at the beginning or end of your working day.

Stage 3: Pessimism

If you maintain the schedule we have outlined above you should succeed in getting a job before you ever reach the pessimistic stage of the unemployment process. However, some people quickly launch themselves into the pessimistic stage by having unrealistic expectations in the first place. The following quotes are typical of the over-optimistic.

I had been made redundant before, in 1982, and I had got myself fixed up within a week. In fact I went down to the jobcentre on the Monday after I finished and fixed up three interviews there and then. I went to two on the Monday and one on the Tuesday and took the Tuesday one. I was also offered a job from one of the Monday interviews, but the Tuesday firm seemed more stable and in fact I stayed there until I was made redundant this time. I started off as a machine operator and after four years they made me foreman. I knew it wouldn't be quite so easy this time, but I was quite prepared to go back to machine operating again. I wasn't expecting a foreman's job or as much money as I was getting before. I thought I would start again somewhere else and work my way up again. But when I went down to the jobcentre I just couldn't believe it. There was nothing, absolutely nothing. All I knew was engineering and there was nothing at all. I went down every day for three weeks but there was never anything and at the end of the third week, I felt as though I could throw myself under a bus. I thought I would never work again.

Peter, Former Foreman/Machine Operator
now on government retraining course

After I'd finished in the July, I managed to get three job interviews quite quickly. One was from an ad in the local paper and the other two were from the Daily Telegraph. *They were all quite good jobs. One was down in the South-East, but I wouldn't have minded moving, and the other two were nearer home. The one in the South-East was paying a bit more than I'd earned before and the other two were about the same as I'd been getting, well one was slightly more. I went to three interviews in about ten days and then after about two weeks, I got replies from all three on the same* day. One was a rejection, this was one of the local ones, but I didn't mind because the other two were asking me to go for second interviews. I went to the local one the next week and they said they had quite a few people on their shortlist and some of them were away on holiday (this was August), so I probably wouldn't hear for about three weeks. This seemed quite reasonable and I wasn't worried because in fact I was rather enjoying myself at home. I had never had a break at home before and it was an ideal chance to catch up on the gardening and do some painting and decorating. It was nice to do some physical work after spending all those years on the road and in offices.

I went to the second interview down in the South-East shortly after. In fact when I got there it was a bit of a shock. They'd asked me to get there at 10 o'clock, which seemed a bit early considering the journey I had to do, but I hadn't liked to object, but when I walked in the reception room, I found out why. It was one of those group interviews and there were nine other people there. We all went into a conference room and each had to give a presentation of the product and then take part in a group discussion and all go out to lunch together. I was a bit horrified at first and then the old adrenalin got going and I rose to the occasion, so to speak. Over lunch, I got into a long conversation with the Marketing Director, who'd organized the whole thing. It was one of those fork buffet do's, and we got on really well. We were obviously on the same wavelength and he thought so too, because at the end of the day he came over and said they were inviting three people back to meet the Managing Director who would be making the final decision and I was one of them. I was 'over the moon' as they say. I'd been down there twice now and I'd seen a bit of the area and it was lovely. The wife's sister lived about thirty miles away, so the wife was quite keen on the idea and my little boy was just starting his last year at the junior school and would be changing schools anyway the next year so it looked as though a move could fit in very well. Again they'd said there would be a bit of a delay before the final interview because the Managing Director was on holiday, but about ten days later I got a letter inviting me for the final interview in a fortnight's time.

By now, I'd really got my heart set on it and I was really

excited going down on the train, but as soon as I got into the Managing Director's office I knew I wouldn't get it. He was one of those public school types in a pin-stripe suit and the first thing he said to me was, 'I see you haven't got a degree,' not that they'd said anything before about having a degree, and from there things just went from bad to worse. He obviously just didn't like me. I went home feeling very down and to cap it all I found that a rejection had come in the post from one other local job. A few days later I got a rejection letter, a very apologetic one in fact, from the Marketing Director of the other firm. This had all taken about three months altogether and I'd been so certain I'd get one of these jobs that I hadn't bothered applying for others. I felt really let down and messed about and it was about a week before I could gear myself up to starting the whole process all over again.

Graham, Sales and Marketing Manager, aged 42

These two cases illustrate how important it is to be realistic about job hunting. In our job-seeker's timetable, he succeeds in getting one interview per week, and this would be quite good going these days, but he does not immediately drop all other job search activity until he hears the result of his interview. It is unrealistic either to expect to find suitable jobs immediately, to rely heavily on getting any particular job or like Peter to rely on one source of jobs. Job search must be a continuous systematic process until you succeed in your objective. Don't come away all elated from your first job interview believing that you are bound to get the job. If you do get it, that's wonderful, but if you don't you are going to feel much more severely let down if you have been sitting at home waiting on a job offer than if you have been out and about securing yourself other interviews.

Stage 4: Fatalism

Both Peter and Graham felt themselves in danger of stepping into the fatalistic stage of reaction to redundancy when their first job-hunting efforts were unsuccessful, the 'I'm never going to get a job' stage. Both had been over-optimistic about securing a new job and when their early hopes were dashed they felt like giving up. It is important not to expect too much too soon. As we mentioned earlier in the book, 50 per cent of those who become unemployed now take over a year to find another job. When unemployment is high, it does not mean principally that people will not get new jobs, but that it will take them longer to get new jobs. If you conduct your job search in a systematic way and follow the advice in this book you should secure a job long before you start to feel fatalistic about your employment chances. If you live in a particularly difficult area for work and you have not got a new job within a year, it does not mean you should sit back and give up. What you will have to do is to reappraise your situation and examine some of the alternatives to conventional employment. These are outlined in Chapter 7.

This chapter has outlined common reactions to redundancy. If you do have a day when your job-finding hopes seem dim, do not however immediately jump to the conclusion that you are coming out of the optimistic and into the pessimistic stage. We all have our 'off' days and if you maintain your job-hunting activity you will not sink into pessimism. The pessimistic and fatalistic stages start when people stop bothering to look for jobs. The support of your family and friends is also vital in maintaining your optimistic approach to job hunting and this will be examined further in the following chapter.

Chapter 6

Getting Help

Family and Friends: Networking and Support

One of the major sources of support for a redundant person is his or her family and friends. Redundancy is something which can make or break a marriage and it is essential that your family as well as you take a positive attitude to your situation. One of the best ways that they can help you is to read this book. They will then not only understand what you are trying to do, they will also understand some of the problems you are up against. On paper is sounds very simple: 'Of course my family will back me up to the hilt'; but there are sound psychological reasons why they find this more difficult than you or they initially think:

Well it was all right at first. I told my mum and dad what had happened and my dad said he'd ask if there was anything going at his firm and mum said not to bother paying her anything until I'd got myself back in work. The day after I finished I went down the Jobcentre and they fixed me up with a couple of interviews. Then I got the local paper and I got two more interviews out of that. Then my friend who works in Marks and Spencer's office, she got me an interview down there and I was feeling quite chuffed. Anyway, to cut a long story short, I went to all those interviews and I didn't get a single one, not a bloody one (excuse my language). Well after that I stopped looking for a bit and started staying in bed until twelve o'clock. Then my mum came home early one

*day because she didn't feel very well and she found me still
in bed. We had a blazing row and she said I was a lazy good-
for-nothing and when my dad came home he started on me
and I was that fed up I walked out of the house and went
round to my friend's and didn't go back for two days.*

Clerk/typist, aged 21

With the best will in the world, it is very hard for the family
to be supportive when the redundant person is doing
nothing to help themselves. If they can see you are doing
all you can, they will have a much better attitude. Also
where you are the sole breadwinner, your partner will be
very worried about the situation. If your partner is not used
to having you at home, she will not only feel worried, she
will also feel her routine is being disrupted, and this is one
of the reasons why it is better to do some of your job
hunting out of the home.

The way in which other people react to your redundancy
is important for maintaining your self-esteem and
unfortunately they may not react in the most positive way.
Psychologists talk about the problem of 'attribution biases'.
What this means quite simply is that whilst people
themselves believe their misfortunes are the result of
external circumstances, other people will often think they
are the person's own fault. The implications of this for
you as a redundant person are that whilst you will feel
that your redundancy came about for example, because
the company had to cut back staff due to lack of orders,
other people will think there must have been some reason
why the company chose to single you out. Perhaps you
weren't a very good worker? Similarly, whilst you may
think that you have not yet got a job because there are not
many jobs available, other people will think that you have
not got a job because you haven't been trying hard enough.
These attributional biases affect our thinking without our
being aware of it and it is very important for the family and
friends of redundant people to guard against this sort of
negative attitude. It is also important for redundant people
not to be too upset if they do meet with such reactions.
People are not being deliberately offensive, they just can't
help it and if you think back over how you reacted to
redundant people when you were still employed, you may

remember thinking similar things about them.

Family and friends can help you psychologically by taking a positive attitude to your situation. What help can they give you practically? We have already mentioned that many jobs are obtained through personal contacts and you should therefore enlist the help of all your family and friends as job-spotters. Ask them to keep their eyes and ears open at their own firms, in their local press if it is different from yours, in job agencies' windows if they have access to different ones from you, and also amongst their friends. Again this is all part of the networking process.

Although you can undertake some of your job-hunting activities out of the house, your job hunting will inevitably intrude into the home. Many employers will contact you by telephone rather than by letter if they want to interview you, so make sure the family is briefed on how to answer the telephone in a polite and efficient manner. Have a pad and pen ready by the telephone with a note of what information they should get from the caller: name, company, telephone number, when it would be convenient to call back and a message if the caller wants to leave one. Leave a note of what time you expect to be back in the house in case people want to call you back. A secretary friend of ours was told by her future boss that he was so impressed by her children's beautiful telephone manner, that before she came to the interview he was convinced she must be the right person for the job.

You are not likely to get a job solely on the strength of how your family answer the telephone, but it all helps in creating the right impression to a future employer. If you have ever thought of investing in an answering machine, this could be a good time to do it if you have some spare redundancy cash. You can then go out without having to worry about missing important calls.

Some of your application letters will also have to be written at home and you will need to keep files of correspondence, job advertisements, company information etc. If you have a partner with secretarial skills, and access to a word processor or a typewriter, this is a great help. Employers prefer typewritten letters because they look more business-like and are easier to read. If your partner is a better letter-writer than you, ask him or her to draft your application letters for you, and then copy them out.

We have suggested some ways in which your family and friends can help you when you are redundant and also some ways they can avoid being unhelpful. What other sources of help and support are there?

Fee-Charging Services

Vocational Guidance

There are two major types of careers advice agencies; those who give vocational guidance and those who actively help you find a job. You may be interested in the services of either or both depending on your particular circumstances.

The vocational guidance counsellors offer a psychological testing service that will test your intelligence, aptitudes, personality and interests and will follow this up with an in-depth interview with a psychologist who will ask you about your family background, educational history, career history and present circumstances. The interview will be longer and will cover more personal issues than a job interview and the emphasis is on helping you to find out more about yourself. Unlike a job interview you are not trying to impress anyone and you should be as truthful as you possibly can. Many job-seekers have a prepared spiel which describes the successes of their career history and carefully omits all the failures such as, for instance, that job you started in 1982 where you were fired on the fourth day or the fact that you started studying for A-levels but left in the first term because you couldn't keep up. Also most people are used to being asked in job interviews why they took a particular job and have a pat answer which is designed to convince future employers that they always wanted to be a lavatory attendant, that they love being a lavatory attendant and that they will always want to be a lavatory attendant, or whatever job it is that they go after. Whereas in a job interview you may not tell an employer that you became an electrician because it was the only apprenticeship you could get, your dad said you had to get an apprenticeship, and that you loathe being an electrician, this is the sort of information that the psychologist will want to know. Don't present the 'rationalized' version of your career purely out of force of habit.

During the course of the interview the psychologist will also discuss the test results with you and tell you the sort of job that they indicate you could do. The interest tests will indicate certain areas of work such as that which involves using figures and numbers, or involves selling things and ideas to people, or work involving a manual skill. Having an interest in a particular area does not necessarily mean that you have any aptitude for that type of work or the ability to do any particular job in that area of work. The intelligence test will indicate the level at which you are likely to be able to work and whether you are a potential skilled employee, technician, manager etc. The aptitude tests will indicate whether you have the type of intelligence necessary for particular occupations. Do you have the high level of verbal intelligence necessary for literary work? Do you have the high level of visuo-spatial ability needed by an architect or construction engineer? The personality test is an additional guide to the type of work and working environment most likely to suit you. If you are a dedicated introvert, you will not enjoy knocking on doors selling double-glazing, and if you are a people-loving extrovert, you will not want to spend all day sitting alone in a room at the end of a computer terminal.

The tests and interview will allow you and the psychologist to build up a picture of the sort of person you are and the type of job which is likely to suit you. If you have been happy in the work you were doing in the past and are likely to be able to continue in this line, you are not likely to need this type of service. The people who will benefit are those who were unhappy in their former jobs or cannot continue in them. If this is the case, now may be the ideal opportunity to change direction. Your redundancy may have come about as the result of a decline in demand for your particular expertise. If you are an unemployed miner or steelworker, you are unlikely to find re-employment in these declining industries. Career change can therefore be a voluntary change or one which is forced upon you.

Careers Counselling

Vocational guidance counsellors will not help you find a new job. This is the forte of the careers counsellors or outplacement consultants. The function of careers counsellors is to help you sell yourself on the job market. They cannot guarantee to get you a job, they can only put you in the best possible position to do so. The service they offer will usually include in-depth interviews to enable you and they to identify your strengths and weaknesses, and assistance in preparing a CV that highlights those strengths and presents your career in the most positive light. Some companies when preparing your CV use a particular 'house style'. For reasons which are discussed further below, it is best to avoid having your CV prepared in one of the companies' standardized formats.

Having assessed your strengths and weaknesses, the careers counsellor will advise you on the type of job you should seek, the salary you can hope to get and the types of company you should approach. Careers counsellors favour making speculative approaches to companies, as well as applying to specific advertisements. Some will suggest to you which companies to approach and will leave it to you to make the contact; others will undertake to send your CV to the company on your behalf. Many companies compile a monthly brochure of the clients on their books, whom they identify by reference number only, and they circulate this to large companies and selection and search consultancies. Some careers counsellors also offer testing and guidance services which can help you to make decisions about career change, or you could seek such advice a vocational guidance specialist first and then go to a careers counsellor to help you find a different type of job.

Pros and Cons of the Different Services

Vocational Guidance

Vocational guidance is unlikely to be of interest unless you are contemplating some kind of distinct change in the type of employment you are seeking. If you are contemplating such a change, then the services they can offer can be invaluable. They can tell you whether or not you have the necessary qualities to make you successful in a new line of work and prevent your making a disastrous mistake. If they do back up your own judgement, you will have a big psychological boost to help you through what could be a difficult transition of establishing yourself in a different career.

Vocational guidance usually takes a day. A normal format would be for you to take the tests in the morning, have lunch while these are marked and then have an interview with a psychologist in the afternoon. Alternatively you may visit the establishment on two separate half-days. Most vocational guidance organizations are based in London, although some of the large ones have facilities outside the capital. If you have to travel to London from a distance in order to visit their premises, then to reduce the expense it is best to choose a firm which will carry out the complete service on one day. The names of some of the better known consultancies are included in Chapter 9. Others are listed in the Yellow Pages under 'Careers Advice'. When choosing a consultant, shop around. Ask them to send you copies of their brochures and compare what they are offering. Fees vary widely and the higher fee does not necessarily mean better service, as some are non-profit-making organizations. This is information that you will be able to glean from the brochures. Your employer may well be willing to pay the fees for you and may in any case be able to recommend a firm to you. Many vocational guidance consultancies also undertake psychological testing for companies when they are recruiting and your personnel department may therefore have contacts with these organizations.

Careers Counsellors

Careers counsellors deal almost exclusively with those at the top end of the job market; middle managers and up. You may not therefore be able to avail yourself of their services. Like vocational guidance counsellors, many are London-based. Opinions about the worth of their services vary considerably. Unfortunately the executive redundancy market is an area which a number of people have chosen to cash in on in recent years and many executives have been talked into parting with large sums of money to very little effect by unscrupulous people. Careers counselling is very expensive in comparison with vocational guidance. Consultants will not guarantee to find you a job. In fact the more inflated their promises, the less reputable they are likely to be and you should avoid like the plague anyone who does make you such a promise. Whatever the individual consultancy's fees, you are talking about thousands of pounds of your money. Is it worth it?

Many of the things careers counsellors can do for you, you can also do for yourself, and some of the guidance they can give can be obtained from other sources. Your company's personnel department can advise you on CV writing and interview and job-hunting techniques. Free advice is also obtainable from such organizations as job clubs and unemployed people's self-help groups. The help which these organizations can provide is explained below. If you would have to pay for the service yourself, it may therefore be better to take advantage of these free resources and to put your redundancy money to other uses. Psychologically, it is also better to undertake your own job hunting than to allow someone else to do it for you. As we have explained earlier, it is important in redundancy to take control of your life and to make things happen yourself rather than to allow things to happen to you. The better careers counsellors will not encourage you to become overdependent on them, but will encourage you to do things for yourself, however tempting it is to sit back and allow someone else to do all the work.

We mentioned that it is unwise to let careers counsellors prepare your CV in their house style. The counsellors have an image among recruiters which they are trying to live down, of dealing with executive failures. A survey by CEPEC, one of the major consultancies, found that selection and search consultants in particular had very negative reactions to CVs which were identifiably from careers counsellors. Some careers counsellors will telephone companies and consultancies advertising jobs and recommend you for them. Although they claim their recommendation will assist the candidate, the truth is that this is as likely to produce a negative as a positive reaction.

Other careers counsellors take a less active hand in promoting you on the job market, but instead provide you with facilities to promote yourself. They provide you with space in an office with other redundant executives and you run your job hunting from the office on a 9 to 5 basis, as you would any other full-time job. You are provided with access to telephones, typing facilities, photocopying and company information, and you are given advice on job hunting and interview techniques. In some cases this includes interview training using audio-visual equipment. If you have not previously seen your interview performance on video, this can be a sobering and enlightening experience.

This type of approach to careers counselling which encourages you to market yourself and to treat job hunting as a full-time occupation whilst providing you with the facilities to do it, is vastly preferable to any other approach. It has the psychological benefits of putting you in control of the situation and is likely to maintain you in the optimistic phase of adjustment to redundancy by getting you out of the house and keeping you active. A slight air of competitiveness is also consciously encouraged. When other people around you are getting jobs and interviews, it is a spur to do likewise.

Whether to take advantage of careers counsellors' services depends to a large extent on who is going to be paying. Where you would have to pay for the service yourself, you should think very carefully about the pros and cons. Many of the services and much of the advice provided can be obtained elsewhere and it would be sensible to investigate the free services before committing yourself. When choosing a careers counsellor ask around your personnel department and amongst friends and acquaintances. If you can find someone who has had successful dealings with one of the organizations, then this is obviously the best recommendation. Otherwise ask the consultancies to send you some literature and compare costs and the services which are offered. More and more frequently however companies are paying for the services of careers counsellors as part of the redundancy package. Several of the better known outplacement firms only take people on this basis. If the service is free, then obviously take it, but steer your employer towards a consultancy providing facilities for you to do your own job hunting, rather than the 'we will sell you on the job market' approach.

Self-Help Groups

Whilst executives are well provided for as far as job-hunting advice is concerned, there is little provision for those at the non-executive end of the job market. This is unfortunate because the recruitment process has become more sophisticated at all levels and for even the simplest job you will need to know how to fill in application forms, how to write yourself a CV which you can send on spec to employers, and how to behave at job interviews. This book sets out all the information you need, but it is always useful to have someone else to check that your CV does not contain any spelling mistakes and to help you practise your interview technique.

To assist with this the Department of Employment has set up a system of Job Clubs for anyone who has been out of work for 6 months or more. They will give you free advice on how to apply for jobs and they will provide free stamps and stationery and the use of typewriters, photocopiers, newspapers and business directories. They will pay your fares to attend the club and they claim a high record of success (over 50 per cent) in getting people into jobs.

As unemployment has increased over recent years, there has been a mushrooming of organizations of unemployed people, known as self-help groups. These have arisen out of the need of unemployed people for support and encouragement during their period of unemployment. They can provide members not only with job-hunting advice, but also information on the operation of the benefits system and concessions etc. offered to unemployed people. Some operate from members' houses, but others have local authority funding and their own offices. You may wonder whether the company of large numbers of unemployed people could be depressing. In the main, however, the groups are very beneficial and help you to get your problems into perspective by realizing that there are many other people whose situation is worse than yours and that other people have come across the same problems as you and survived.

The main negative aspect to guard against with these groups is that you do not get so involved in the group that you start making a profession of being unemployed and forget about job hunting. Some of the earlier groups were political and had a left-wing bias which may or may not appeal.

On the whole, however, self-help groups provide much-needed advice and support. To find out if there is a group in your area you can contact your local library, jobcentre, Citizens Advice Bureau or look in the lists given in Chapter 9.

Chapter 7
Job Offers and After

Throughout this book we have stressed the need to go into the job hunt in a competitive frame of mind; to apply for a broad range of jobs which either your experience or your inclination suggest are suitable. We have emphasized job winning and from that it may be assumed that we were putting forward a philosophy of 'Never mind the quality, it's a job.'

That has been a valid position to take; relevant up to the point when you are finally offered a job. What then should your reaction be? This chapter analyses what happens from this point, what you should consider and how you should go about ensuring as far as possible that your future works out as you would wish to see it.

With the job offer the relative position between the job-hunter and the prospective employer radically alters. Up to this point you have been the seller, they the buyer; you have been the seeker, they the holders of what you are seeking. Now the situation has changed: they want you.

Your Attitude

How do you react? At all levels of jobs if they are particularly keen they are quite likely to give a verbal offer at your final interview. If they are working through a consultancy they are quite likely to get them to sound you out, to gain an indication of whether you are likely to accept. In both cases they are asking for an immediate reaction; a verbal commitment.

Other companies will do things differently. They will have further candidates to see, they will have to confer. Nevertheless once they have decided they may well telephone you before they choose to make a formal offer to you in writing.

In most cases therefore the likelihood is for an immediate verbal response. Do you take it? It's usually wise to try and play for time in order that you may think things through as comprehensively as possible. You might have felt immediately after the interview that the job was everything you would want it to be but even so, exercise a little caution. Are all the other considerations equally satisfactorily settled? Will the terms and conditions relating to the job be as expected? Will the content of the job actually be as stated in the original ad or during your discussions? Companies, just like individuals, can get over-enthusiastic in the heat of the moment and thus unintentionally oversell the job. What are the career prospects? Do you know all you need to know to make an informed decision?

The following checklist may be of help:

1. *Is the job essentially one that you want?*
   Was it one you would have wanted regardless of redundancy or was it one you applied for out of desperation, to get the ball rolling?

2. *Is it a company for whom you would want to work?*
   Do you know all you need about the company? Is it viable? Would you feel pride in being associated with it?

3. *Will you enjoy working with the people already there?*
   Did you meet all the relevant people in the team? Can you envisage working with them constructively?

4. *Are the prospects good?*
   Are they in line with your thinking? Will you be able to progress within the company gaining promotion or will it provide useful experience to use as a springboard to better jobs outside? Even more importantly, will the job last?

5. *Are the pay and conditions in line with your expectations?*
   Do they continue in line with your previous salary? How do they match up to the responsibilities of the job? Can

they be bettered? What is the review system?

6. *How will it fit in with your domestic circumstances?*
Will you have to relocate? Will this cause problems with your wife/husband? How will this affect your children's schooling? Do you know enough about the area? How do house prices compare? Will the company help with relocation expenses? Will the job itself cause any foreseeable stress on your family, i.e. considerable overseas or UK travel, late-night working, disruptive shift patterns? Are you used to these? How prepared are you to accept them?

7. *Can you do better?*
Have you applied for any other jobs that you would prefer? Will this one stretch you enough and offer you sufficient challenge? Is there a likelihood that better jobs will occur within a reasonable time frame? What is the likelihood of being offered them? If you are currently considering any other possibilities are these better? Is it worth the gamble to hold out and see what else transpires?

This last question really is the crux of the matter, whether those exciting bird(s) in the bush are worth risking against the bird in the hand. What *could be* can always appear more interesting and simply better than what *is*. Against that however what if those opportunities don't develop as planned? After all, you have no guarantee that they will. Could you stand starting from scratch again? Are you prepared to go through the whole process again? Do you have the mental reserves and the stamina for this?

The answer of course is one that only you can decide. It will depend very much on you, the job and your circumstances. If for example the job offer is not only the first but has come round very quickly since your redundancy you might feel inclined to hang on a little longer. As the length of your out-of-work period grows, there is obviously much greater sense in taking whatever is on offer.

The Company's Attitude

Often companies aren't as sympathetic as they might be in this situation. They have decided they want you and they know you want a job. Any caution on your part may therefore smack of indecision in their eyes, which is obviously the last impression you want to make. It is worth being cautious however as some less scrupulous companies may offer you rather less than their advertisement indicated, or a less favourable benefit package simply because they assume that, being in need of a job, you will take second best.

Similarly when recruiting for less-skilled jobs, where perhaps the skills and experience required to do the job are more widespread, companies can be quite heavy-handed. 'Do you accept? Because I have six others in the list who I can call.' Nothing we have come across within commercial companies however comes near the method of recruiting teachers and also some local authority staff, where all are interviewed on the same day and sit in a waiting room together while the decision is reached. The name of the successful candidate is called, the person is called into the room where the offer is made and which must be accepted or turned down by the candidate then and there. If that candidate accepts, the others are sent home. If the offer is rejected then number two candidate is called in and so on, with anyone who turns the job down sometimes not getting their expenses reimbursed. Accepting the job but turning it down later may entail you being blacklisted by that local authority as far as future jobs are concerned. It is not a happy situation and is surprisingly still current.

Normally, though, you will be allowed time to think. If the pressure is on, whether fairly or unfairly applied, it is better to accept verbally and then consider carefully before signing anything. This is perhaps one of the few times where self-interest has to come first: where you have to look after Number One. You cannot afford to make the wrong decision.

In some situations, especially with unskilled jobs, the employers will have insisted on an immediate decision and, on acceptance, insist you start almost immediately. Again it is better to play along, go through with it and see how it works out. The whole job-seeking exercise needn't stop there however; if better opportunities come up, explore them to their fullest extent and if they are better, take them. This applies to all levels of the job market. This is the best chance you are likely to have to make the most of your future and it is really up to you to seize that chance.

Negotiation

Usually when you accept a job offer, or immediately prior to doing so, the company will expect some degree of negotiation of terms. Obviously in the public sector and in some of the larger companies the job will be graded within clear parameters, and so flexibility in what they pay you is limited. Often, however, they will have a separate entry scale and it is sometimes possible, because of your particular blend of skills and experience, to raise yourself a couple of notches on this.

With private sector companies the situation is much more varied. What you get will largely be determined in negotiations between you and the company. To a certain extent this will boil down to an equation: how much they want you as opposed to how much you want. But even with this, other factors will come into play. How much others in the company on a similar reporting level receive will certainly influence the decision. Paying you more than those already there is a classic way of breeding resentment and disharmony. Similarly market forces will come into play. The degree of competition for the job will certainly affect how flexible they are prepared to be.

You will also be in a less strong position as far as negotiation is concerned than someone still in employment. Companies will not usually go so far to meet terms as they would for somebody they felt needed to be enticed out of another job. The important things to be aware of therefore are:

- Is it a fair rate for the job and well within the advertised range? Make sure they are not trying to get you on the cheap.
- Does the benefit package live up to expectations? How comparable is it to your previous job? Can it be

improved? There is often much more flexibility here than in terms of pure salary.

• How will the total deal affect your living standards? Will, for example, extra travel negate most of the improvement in income?

When terms are agreed try to get them in writing well before you start work. Although there is a legal requirement for a written contract, it doesn't have to be supplied for up to three months after you have started work, when obviously your negotiating strength is seriously weakened. Do also check that everything you have negotiated is included in your contract as it is often very difficult to remedy things after the event. Get them right before you start.

All this might seem somewhat academic to someone who is desperate to get a job. There is nothing so galling and frustrating however once the initial euphoria of landing a job has worn off as to realize that as far as the remuneration package is concerned you could have done much better and all those promises of various perks never seem to materialize.

If you feel negotiation is difficult because of the weakness of your position, i.e. you need a job and thus feel unable to dictate terms, then a very useful item to build into your contract is the early review date. With this you accept their terms but stipulate that after three or six months these will be reviewed in the light of your performance. This can certainly put you in a strong negotiating position. Firstly you have proved your worth; they can now appreciate your value to their company; and secondly if you are contributing they will automatically prefer to pay you more rather than risk losing you and be made to go through the entire expensive and time-consuming process of recruitment again.

What to Accept

We stressed earlier that in the early days of the job search it was advisable to apply for as many different jobs as possible: firstly to get the momentum going, secondly to get much-needed interview practice and thirdly to get into a position of being offered jobs it is often necessary to look wider than if you were still employed.

What happens however when the first offer is something at a lower level than you have previously been doing, when it is not a job you really want? This is of course a tremendously difficult question on which to give guidance on a hypothetical level, as the situations to which it relates can be very variable. By and large one might be best advised, especially if nothing better seems to be coming up quickly, to take the position but regard it as a stepping stone, a means to an end. Remember, it is much easier to find a job if you already have one than if you need one. Take the job but continue the search.

To this general rule must be added a warning. The longer you work in a lower-level job the harder it will be to convince people that you are capable of holding a job at a higher level. A works director, for example, may well find that, by taking a job as a production supervisor, he will after a period be assumed capable of doing only a job at that level or at one notch above, i.e. production manager. For about six months a lower-level job can be regarded as a temporary expedient which has the advantages of demonstrating your motivation to work. After that it will tend to be seen as a permanent career move and people will think you are not capable of doing much more and assume that this was why you were made redundant in the first place.

What too if the job offer is with a company which, as far as you have been able to establish, isn't trading too successfully at the moment, or is in a declining market sector? Alternatively they might be making people with skills different from your own redundant, or they may have a justified reputation for overmanning.

It is easy to give solutions in general terms: avoid any companies which seem to fit into the categories given above, gravitate towards companies which are more likely to be successful in the current economic climate or in the future; the so-called 'sunrise' industries perhaps – but this might involve relocation. As far as jobs are concerned, go for the ones which are essential to a company or where overmanning is least likely – but this might involve retraining. Meanwhile you've been offered a job which you can do and would enjoy doing but with a company whose future, either in terms of its products or by the way it's managed, doesn't look too bright. What should you do?

Again, we can't be categoric in our answer. Rather it depends on a complicated series of equations which boil down to whether the short-term advantages outweigh the long-term prospects. In many cases the answer may be a resounding yes and, if so, there's no problem. You might even be moving into a position in which you can actively contribute to the company's recovery. A high risk perhaps, but one you may decide is well worth it. Alternatively you may decide that anything concrete to enable you to pay the bills is better than living in hope; so be it.

Ideally, though, it is worth giving thought to the long term. Most people will be looking for a job which will last and will provide some kind of career progression. In that way the security of the family can be maintained. The best way to achieve this is of course to take the longer view and go firstly for jobs in companies which seem to be expanding, whose future looks secure. Secondly go for jobs in those companies whose products will either be always in demand or, because of breakthroughs in technology will become increasingly in demand, rather than companies whose products will be superseded by technological advances.

Not many of us however can make that transition without retraining. This we discuss in a later chapter. What can be done however is pick the good companies and, if possible, go for the jobs which have to be regarded as essential and thus run least risk of redundancy. If you are doing an essential job and you are the only person doing it, you are much less likely to become redundant as opposed to the situation where you are one of many doing essentially the same job. Management are much more likely to try and streamline that situation to save costs than dispense with the services of their only accountant, their only fitter or whatever.

The Benefit Package

As you are no doubt aware, in most jobs nowadays the remuneration package is not simply composed of a salary or wage. Included in the package will be a whole host of 'extras' such as a pension, luncheon vouchers or other means of subsidizing your meals such as a free canteen, bonus payments, car, expenses, and possibly life and health cover, loan facilities and help with relocation. At most senior levels there may well be a share option scheme.

Do make sure you know precisely what is on offer and that it is actually put into your contract. As we have mentioned, if you are moving into a job for which a definite salary scale has been worked out, you can often increase your overall package by selective negotiation on some of these 'fringe' benefits. Do make sure however they are in your contract, as it is quite common to find that having negotiated a special deal with one individual on a verbal basis this is often not fully communicated to the clerk in the Company Secretary's or Personnel Department who sends you out the standard contract. Once signed, it will be far more difficult to negotiate.

In summary therefore in appraising the merits of a job offer, remember that the balance has shifted. Instead of being the seeker you are now the sought-after. Think the offer through coolly and carefully. Judge it against other potential offers and their likelihood of coming up. Negotiate for the best possible deal, but be realistic about this, keep well within the dividing line between wanting to do as well as possible as opposed to creating an impression of sheer greed. Finally measure the effect the job will have on you and your family.

Remember too that while we are advocating caution and the coolly balanced appraisal of the situation, you might well be under tremendous pressure from the company to reach a quick decision. Obviously you can't keep them hanging on indefinitely and it's not in your career interests to appear either indecisive and/or obdurate. Try and decide as quickly as possible; within two or three days at most. If in doubt take the job but quietly continue the search.

Changing Status: Unemployed to Employed

There are lots of little but important things to do in the lead-up time to the first day back at work. For, as we have previously suggested, getting a job is a full-time job in itself and, as you will know on leaving a job, there are countless things to be done in order to tidy up all the loose ends.

Signing Off

Do remember to do this properly. In these days of fortnightly signing there can be quite a gap between your last signing day and the day you actually start work. Fill in the UB40 form as fully as possible, giving full details of when and where you will be starting work and send it to the Benefit Office or drop it in personally. They should then work out how much benefit you are entitled to up to the point of starting work and send you a giro, together with a new P45 and a statement of how much taxable benefit you have received. Do make sure you fill it in properly, for, as we have mentioned before, you should never give them an opportunity to delay your entitlement on a bureaucratic technicality.

Similarly with the DSS office. Let them know when and where you intend to start work. As their criterion is for payment based on need rather than on what you have previously paid into the system, their method of dealing with your signing off is different from that of the Benefit Office. They will be more interested in when you will be paid by your new employer. Should this be some time away, if for example, you are to be paid monthly in arrears, you can ask them to give you an interim payment to keep you going until the first pay cheque.

Letting People Know

To start up your job hunt we recommend contacting as many people as possible to let them know you were job hunting. Not only is it courteous to let all the consultancies, agencies, friends, relatives and business contacts know when you have attained your goal, it can be very useful as well. It obviously makes sense to let your trade contacts and acquaintances know. After all they may be inclined to put business in your new firm's way now they know you'll be there to handle it, but let all the others know as well. Apart from giving your ego no end of a well and hard-earned fillip, it does pay to keep in touch. Tell the agencies and consultancies whether you see the job being an interim move or permanent and whether you wish to remain on their books. You are now a more easily marketable commodity in their eyes and who knows what that might bring? If you're in the type of job likely to interest a head-hunter, then they might well want to keep you on file not only as a source of advice but also after a decent period as a potential candidate for more senior roles. Similarly this job might just not work out and it pays to have cultivated a good, relaxed and positive relationship with the job handlers.

Getting Ready for the Start

If you do have any time between accepting the job and starting, do use it as constructively as you can. Build on the research you have done to get the job by working out how you are actually going to cope in the position. In short, switch your thinking from the hypothetical to the actual. What do you plan to do in the job, what will you want to do first and what will you need to know once there to enable you to do it successfully?

Similarly, work out the logistics in getting to the job. If you are relocating, what help will the company give you in finding temporary accommodation? Make sure you're booked in somewhere and the reservation confirmed as far in advance as possible. Decide with your wife or husband whether you plan to move the family as quickly as possible or whether you plan to commute on a weekly basis until you are satisfied the job will work out as planned. An important factor to take into consideration on this might be your children's education. Are they at a critical stage? Is it better to move them now or hold off a while?

If you decide to move straight away, spend as much time as you can getting to know the new area and activate all the local estate agents so that they are working for you. House moving is a long, awesome, tense and emotional business, and coupled with the strangeness of a new job and its inbuilt challenge it can be a great strain. If your wife or husband can take some of this strain off you, all well and good. Otherwise it might be better managed if you can defer it a little while up to such time as you feel reasonably settled into your new job.

In the majority of cases a house move won't be necessary, but do still work out how you will get to work on a regular basis. You will have visited the company site at least once and probably more, so you will know how to get there. Do be aware though of the time difference in travelling during the rush hour. Your interviews may well have taken place outside the morning and evening cram so take this into account. Nothing creates a worse impression than late arrival on your very first day.

The other things to do during this time are really the same as your mother made you do before going back to school after the summer holidays. Make sure you start off on the right foot by having whatever you intend wearing cleaned, pressed and repaired and your shoes polished. If you have to provide equipment for the job, make sure you've got it and that it's all in working order. Finally get all visits to dentists, hairdressers and perhaps doctors out of the way. All this will create a good impression when you start. You will not want to create doubts about your motivation by taking time off for such things in your first few weeks. Do remember, too, to get out your P45 ready for the first day. Just as in the interview, first impressions are vital. It is much more easy to build on, or at least maintain a good impression than it is to counteract, reverse or remedy getting off on the wrong foot.

Back in Work

You're now back in business and starting to get to grips with the job. You've got through all the first-day hassle. You've arrived on time, you've gone through all the personnel details, filling in endless forms which seem to be just rewrites of your original application form. You've met countless different people, probably only remembering a tiny percentage of their names and what they do. You've even remembered to produce your P45, and so they should be able to avoid putting you on emergency income tax coding. Because you're paid in arrears you've seen the person to whom you report and they've promised to try and arrange a 'sub' or cash advance so you've got some money to help you going till pay day. Everything is fine. But how do you avoid getting into the trauma of redundancy again?

Let's assume it's a job you enjoy doing and you like the company. You are looking to make a long-term commitment to stay. How can you make yourself indispensable? The advice below should help.

Make sure you are on top of your job

Make sure you understand all facets of it, the whys and the wherefores; the problems and how to solve them. Make sure your understanding of the job is absolutely in line with company expectations. If in doubt about any area or simply if you don't know how to do a certain part of the job: admit it and seek guidance or training from the person to whom you report. Get it right from day one and don't be afraid to ask your superiors or colleagues if you're not sure. They know you're new and don't expect you to be 'au fait' with everything. The worst possible thing you can do is to pretend to know it all when you don't. They'll find out later and that will erode your position. Getting it straight in the early days shouldn't damage their impression of you at all.

Fit in with them

Get accepted by your colleagues and superiors. Be as helpful and co-operative as possible while making sure your own job gets done.

Make positive suggestions

You will be seeing what they take for granted with fresh eyes. Your previous company might have done the same type of thing and in your view more effectively. Don't be shy about making positive suggestions. A word of warning though: do be balanced and methodical about this. Some of their practices might not only be different from what you are used to, they might also be better. Don't go overboard and try to turn their method of operation into an identikit version of your previous company. Use your common sense: suggest changes which improve efficiency not change for change's sake.

Make yourself indispensable

This is another point where it is difficult to get the question of degree right. You need to build up a reputation of others saying 'I don't know how we managed before we took on Harry', rather than 'That bloody Harry, he's always meddling in things which don't concern him.' When in doubt, stick to your job, making sure you're doing that well but be receptive and positive when your thoughts and comments are invited.

Gravitate towards more secure positions
Once in a company, at whatever level, you will soon be able to establish which jobs seem to be in greater areas of growth than perhaps your own and which therefore might well prove more secure on a long-term basis. If a particular department is growing fast it may well need more staff. Most companies have a policy of recruiting from within whenever possible. If this is the case in your company and the job sounds interesting, apply for it. If you get it, not only will you get some company-provided training in a new skill which will increase the company's investment in you and thus make them less willing to lose you, you will also be increasing your 'employability factor' should you need to move on from that company. You will be adding to your portfolio of skills. Similarly, take advantage of all training schemes provided by your new company even if it is not part of a planned progression into a new job area. Accept everything which will add to or sharpen up your skills. It all helps to making you more employable.

Finally, give a helping hand to others who are still unemployed. It sounds so obvious as to be not worth mentioning, but research has shown that a large proportion of people back in work after a period of redundancy, instead of sympathizing with current sufferers, do all they can to distance themselves from their plight. Because you found the experience worrying, unpleasant, perhaps even distasteful, it is a natural inclination to resent anyone or anything which reminds you of it. You close your mind to it and thus close the door on anyone in that situation.

This is an instinctive reaction but one which we hope you can overcome – especially if you have moved into a position where you can provide positive help, a head of a department, function or section, or if you are in personnel. In any of these roles you may well be required to be involved in the company's recruitment procedures. If so, do try and regard redundant applicants positively on their merits rather than be prejudiced or biased against them. As you know yourself from personal experience, unemployed doesn't mean 'unemployable'.

Similarly, you may well be put in a position where you may eventually have to make people redundant. Do all you can to institute a good redundancy practice within your company. Remember what it was like for you and how it could have been made a lot easier. Try and adopt these practices and procedures and make the whole exercise as positively oriented as possible offering all the help, encouragement and advice that we have outlined throughout the book. Above all 'Do as you would be done by' rather than adopting the easiest way (for you) or the way it was handled previously when you were made redundant.

Chapter 8

Alternatives to Conventional Re-Employment

Most people who are made redundant want to get the same or similar work to that which they had before. Some people, however, will be unable or unwilling to return to their previous type of employment and will be looking for a career change. Some alternatives to the conventional pattern of re-employment are now considered. You may also wish to consider some of these to tide you over a period of unemployment.

Self-Employment

For some people, redundancy and a redundancy payment can be a golden opportunity to set themselves up in business. Self-employment might be in the same field as you worked in before or in an entirely different field, perhaps building on what was previously a hobby. When should you consider self-employment? If there are few job opportunities in your area and you are unwilling to relocate, you may have little alternative. Perhaps you have always wanted to be your own boss, but have lacked the finance or impetus to hive off on your own. These are both good reasons for starting up on your own.

To start up in business on your own you will need both practical and psychological resources. Let us examine the practical resources first. To start your own business you will require money. Money will be needed for premises, even if only to buy furniture for a room in your own house, equipment and stock, publicity and your own living expenses until you start to receive payments. Many small businesses founder because they are inadequately financed and nothing is more frustrating than to have to close down with a drawerful of orders because you cannot meet a few outstanding bills. Before you spend any money you must obtain sound financial advice. The Government is keen to encourage small businesses and there are various publicly-funded schemes to help you.

The Small Firms Service of the Department of Employment provides a free telephone enquiry service and in-depth counselling throughout Great Britain to people who are hoping to set up in business. Dial 0800 222999 and ask for Freefone Enterprise. The service is usually free but a fee may be charged for unusually complicated or lengthy advice. Another government organization is the Rural Development Commission. This organization can provide not only information and advice, but also access to finance and credit. Contact the RDC on 0722 336255. Special help is available in inner cities as part of the Government's 'Action for Cities' programme. Contact the Inner Cities Unit at the Department of Trade and Industry on 071-215 4330, and the Action for Cities Unit at the Department of Environment on 071-276 3053. There are also Urban Development Corporations in certain areas which can provide help in renting premises and training, telephone 071-276 4488. In addition, many local authorities offer services to businesses in their area. There is also a network of over 400 independent, privately-run Local Enterprise Agencies, and in Scotland, Enterprise Trusts, which can offer business advice and counselling. In Scotland, help can also be obtained from the Scottish Development Agency: contact 041-248 2700. In Wales, the Welsh Development Agency is on 0222 22666.

The government also runs courses on self-employment and setting up in small business. Information on these is available from jobcentres and from your local Training and Enterprise Council (TEC). These courses will evaluate your self-employment ideas and assess whether they are realistic and feasible; teach you how to run the financial side of your business; and help you prepare a systematic business plan. TECs and jobcentres can also tell you about the Enterprise

Allowance Scheme. This scheme provides a small government allowance of around £40 per week for a year while you are starting up your business. Eligibility rules vary in different areas, but you must have £1,000 of your own money or £1,000 in the form of a guaranteed loan to put into your business. For a business to be eligible, it must be 'legal, new, based in Great Britain and suitable for support'. Gambling, nude modelling and promoting particular political and religious views are grounds for exclusion! If you are interested you will be invited to attend an information session where the ins and outs of the scheme will be explained.

Banks are another source of finance and often have helpful information packs for small businesses. Banks can also advise you about the Government's Loan Guarantee Scheme by which the Department of Trade and Industry will guarantee 70 to 85 per cent of approved loans over two to seven years in return for a 2 to 5 per cent premium on the guaranteed portion of the loan. The government also has a Business Expansion Scheme. Private investors in your business can claim tax relief on amounts up to £40,000 per year, and this could be an incentive for relatives and friends to invest.

The sources of finance and advice which we have given you above are just a selection of what is available. Local Chambers of Commerce and Enterprise Agencies will be able to suggest further sources of help. Although the economy is not very buoyant at present, never before has so much assistance been available to the small business-person, and if you use available advice and financial assistance wisely, you will be in a good position to become your own boss.

If you want to start your own business, but do not have any specific ideas, you may want to think about franchising. Franchising with reputable companies has a much lower failure rate than other forms of new business and has the advantage that someone else has done much of the ground work and ironed out many of the pitfalls for you. Having bought the franchise, you will normally pay a percentage of turnover to the franchising organization and will have to run your business within guidelines set down. The franchise will be negotiated like a lease, for a set number of years, and at the end of that time will have to be reviewed.

The British Franchise Association is the franchisers' trade association and if you are thinking of buying a franchise you would do well to consider one of its member companies. There are plenty of horror stories of people losing a great deal of money with companies at the more disreputable end of the franchise market. The BFA provides an information pack for a small fee, which contains their membership list, articles about franchising and a check-list of questions to ask a franchiser. Early franchise advertisements included such wonders as the acupuncture franchise which offered to set up franchises in the business as acupuncturists after only a few weeks' training: a normal training course takes four years. Need we say more? The motto when considering a franchise must be to use your common sense. Do not be swayed by over-exaggerated claims, and insist on meeting people who have been successfully trading in a particular franchise for some time before committing yourself. Ask yourself whether you would use the service yourself. If you do not believe in the value of a product or service, it is very difficult to sell it.

Self-employment requires psychological as well as practical qualities. Not everyone is cut out for self-employment, and many people are unprepared for the stresses, strains and loneliness of being their own boss. Self-employment requires self-reliance, self-discipline and self-confidence. If you are the sort of person who needs praise and encouragement from others, the sort of person who finds it difficult to knuckle down to work or lacks the confidence to go out and sell your product and service, then self-employment is not for you. Whether you are a freelance management consultant, home hairdresser or hamburger franchisee, you will have to persuade other people to use your services and convince potential investors that you are a good investment. Your services, however good, will not sell themselves, and you will need to have the ability to create good customer relations if you are to succeed. Self-employment is also unadvisable if you are an anxious person. Cash-flow is a perpetual problem of the small business and you will find yourself constantly in the position of fending off your creditors because of late payment from your debtors. This financial balancing act is not the best way of life for those with weak nerves. Self-employment is often lonely and if companionship at work is important to you, you may be better advised to remain an employee.

If you are contemplating self-employment examine it from all angles. Have you a practical proposition? Can you find adequate financial back-up and have you got the right personality?

Self-employment can also be a temporary measure to tide you over a period of unemployment. If you have a skill and contacts, you may be able to generate some freelance work which will keep you away from the dole queue until you can get yourself permanent employment. When attending job interviews, employers will be more impressed by your having found some way of supporting yourself whilst job hunting than they will by your being unemployed. Look around your local area and see if there are any services you could provide at little outlay.

Career Change

You may have always felt that you were in the wrong job, but lacked the impetus to change. You may have definite ideas about an alternative career, or just a feeling that you are in the wrong environment. If you are unsure about your future direction, career guidance should be considered.

In some types of work, a mature outlook and previous experience in a different area of work can be an asset rather than a handicap. The helping professions prefer people to have some experience of life's problems before they embark on a career of helping others. Although many training courses require formal educational qualifications for younger people, others may be waived in part or entirely for the mature student. Social work, youth work, probation and careers officer work all come into this category.

If you feel you no longer wish to practise your skill or profession, would you enjoy teaching it? Again, entry requirements can be flexible for adults, and if you associate teaching solely with large comprehensive classes of unmanageable teenagers, then think again. Many people do not feel drawn towards teaching children, but would enjoy passing on their knowledge and skill to older people who actively want to acquire it. As a cookery or accountancy lecturer, or whatever your skills happens to be, you can teach in colleges of further or higher education or in evening classes, as well as in schools.

Some branches of the health professions also welcome older applicants. Psychology prefers its clinical practitioners to have some work and life experience behind them before embarking on clinical training. Osteopathy similarly welcomes more mature applicants who have greater ability to inspire confidence in patients than those straight from school and college.

If you are thinking of a career change, then think about areas of work where demand is likely to remain stable or to increase. All kinds of services and also craft skills show a steady increase in demand. As well as social and medical services, the growth of interest in the home has created a steady demand for good craftsmen, carpenters, plumbers, painters and decorators, interior designers, etc. Increasingly, people have tired of poor-quality mass-produced goods and have the money and inclination to pay more for good-quality products ranging from handmade shoes to jewellery, candles, soaps and furniture. Conversely, there are some professions and occupations where you are unlikely to succeed in gaining an entry. Computing and advertising, for instance, are both areas which are over-populated by young, bright graduates. Older and less-qualified people need not apply.

Further Education and Training

If you want to change your career direction or if you want to improve your job chances in your present occupation, you may want to consider gaining further education and training. For degree courses and full-time professional courses, grants are available from your local authority. Some courses such as teaching and degree studies carry mandatory awards. Providing the college or university accepts you and you have not previously held an award, you should be eligible for financial assistance. As well as the basic grant, you may be eligible for additional finance if you have had work experience and/or you are over a certain age. When there is a shortage of skilled people in a particular occupation, a higher rate of grant may be given to encourage people to take up training. Information on courses is available from the relevant professional bodies. Their addresses can be obtained from careers guides in your local library. Information about degree courses at universities can be obtained from the University Central Council on Admissions (UCCA) or the polytechnic equivalent.

Some courses may receive only discretionary awards. Courses such as osteopathy which are considered less conventional will be looked upon with greater favour by some authorities than others. Whilst some authorities will offer the full award, others will offer only a percentage – commonly 80 per cent, and others will offer nothing at all. To find out your authority's attitude you will have to approach the education department. The college concerned may also be able to give you advice.

Many colleges offer other courses designed to prepare older students for higher education. Completion of such courses is recognized as an entry qualification by many universities and polytechnics. If you are seeking admission to a particular establishment, find out exactly what the entry requirements are before embarking on any prior study. Your local authority is not obliged to fund you for such courses, but many authorities are sympathetic. Generally, the more left-wing your council, the more generous it is likely to be. Local authorities are also not obliged to give you an award if you have previously had one. This can be a problem for career changes, and again you will have to investigate your authority's attitude.

Another source of full-time training finance is the Government's Employment Training Scheme which provides training allowances to people who want to obtain training in a new skill or to improve their present qualifications. A wide range of training is available through Employment Training. Your local TEC will be able to give you more advice.

When considering any type of training, find out what the employment prospects are likely to be once you are trained. Ask what the placing prospects are for people leaving the course and look in newspapers to find out whether jobs are being advertised in that occupation. If there are few job vacancies you may find yourself trained for a job which does not exist.

When should you seek further training? If you want to make a complete career change, you may have little alternative. If your occupation is becoming more and more qualification-conscious, this may be a good time to jump on the bandwagon. If your occupation has undergone considerable technological change, this may be a good time to bring yourself up to date.

Evening Classes and Part-Time Education

If you do not want to commit yourself to a full-time course, then part-time education may be the answer. Once you have been unemployed for three months and providing your part-time courses do not exceed 21 hours including recommended outside study time and you are in theory prepared to give up the course if a job becomes available, you can carry on claiming unemployment benefit whilst studying in the day. Local authorities run a wide variety of part-time courses from those leading to specific educational qualifications to skills such as car maintenance. While you are unemployed it is a good idea to plan to improve your job skills and knowledge. Learning new skills and facts will not only enhance your job prospects but will also keep your brain active. Many classes are also run in the evenings and there are no restrictions on attending these if you are unemployed. Most local authorities reduce or waive fees for the unemployed and the fees are in any event small. Details of classes will be available from your local library or education office.

Temporary Work

If you cannot find a permanent job you may be able to find temporary work, either in your normal occupation or in other, perhaps less-skilled, work. Holding down a temporary job will generally provide you with more cash than state benefits, and when you go for interviews for permanent jobs many employers will be impressed by your willingness to work. Temporary work also has the advantage of keeping you in employment whilst allowing you flexibility to go to interviews, etc. Temporary work can also be very enjoyable. However boring the assignment you are on, the fact that you are in a new environment with a new set of people is a stimulus in itself, and the knowledge that you will not be there for long prevents any job becoming too dreary. Sometimes temporary jobs become permanent jobs. If a company knows your work and a permanent vacancy comes up the 'devil they know' usually seems much more preferable than 'the devil they don't'.

Temporary work is available both from commercial and government sources. The high street agencies all deal in temporary vacancies and the jobs available will vary from accountancy work to secretarial work to warehouse labouring, depending on their speciality. You may be able to get temporary work using skills which you have left behind in your career progression. If you started life as a secretary but have since moved on into management, you could go back to secretarial work on a temporary basis. Temporary agencies should, under the Employment Agencies Act, test your skills. If you have not done any typing for some time, try and find a typewriter to practise on before you visit the agency. If you make a mess of things at the first agency, carry on and visit the others. Hopefully you will have got the hang of things before you run out of agencies! Most firms with temporary vacancies contact the agencies at the end of the week. Thursday and Friday are good days to look for a booking for Monday. Some temporary staff are unreliable and if you visit the agency in the first half hour of Monday morning you may pick up a booking where someone has rung in 'sick'.

Some jobcentres also list temporary vacancies, and temporary work is advertised by agencies and in local newspapers. National newspapers are not usually sources of temporary work because their advertising is too expensive. The maternity leave regulations create long-term temporary appointments. Some mothers elect not to return to their jobs and these turn into permanent appointments. Some occupations have seasonal fluctuations and temporary work will be available to cover peak periods such as Christmas or the sales, or to cover holiday periods. Shops, factories, pubs and the Post Office all provide this type of work. In some tourist areas there will be summer jobs available on tourist facilities.

Voluntary Work

By undertaking voluntary work you not only provide a service to the community, you help enhance your own sense of self-worth and extend your range of skills and experience. While claiming state benefits you are free to engage in voluntary work providing you are willing to take up a job if one becomes available. You should however declare any voluntary work to your Benefit Office which can advise you about your position if any payment is involved.

You can find voluntary work by contacting charities, social services departments, old people's homes, hospitals, etc., in your area. Local authorities often have Volunteers Bureaux which can tell you what kind of voluntary work is available and help to direct you to an organization that can use your talents. Many people feel intimidated about approaching the voluntary organizations because they feel they will not fit in with the 'middle-class do-gooder' image. You do not, however, have to have a middle-class accent or any particular skills or qualifications to volunteer, just a genuine desire to do something useful. If you are thinking of a career change to social or community work, experience of voluntary work will prove your commitment, and will also help you to find out whether you are cut out for such work on a full-time basis.

Emigration

Until recently, emigration was often the answer for the skilled and qualified redundant. Countries such as Australia, New Zealand and Canada had economies which remained stronger than that of the UK, despite worldwide economic problems such as oil shortages and inflation. Their doors have been increasingly closed, however, as they have begun to experience their own economic problems, and emigration has become much more difficult.

Australia, once the haven of NHS-weary doctors, is now interested only in doctors who would be willing to work in the remotest areas, which to most British people seems desperately out of touch with civilization. Australia's immigration is controlled by a points system. Points are given for the amount of capital you have, your job experience and qualifications, the size of your family, your age, health, ability to speak English, whether you have close relatives in the country and a number of other factors. The number of points required before you can be considered is raised and lowered according to the demand for immigrants. The occupations which will be considered vary monthly, and to find out if you are eligible you will need to contact Australia House on a regular basis. Australia has its own growing unemployment problems, and unemployment is currently in excess of UK levels. The immigration authorities may not consider you at all unless you have a relative in the country, but this is something which is again liable to change and you will have to investigate the current situation when you apply.

New Zealand now welcomes only immigrants who have guaranteed jobs, but Canada is willing to consider those with specific skills. South Africa is most in need of immigrants because of the annual outflow of those who now find the political situation too unstable. Regardless of your opinion of the South African regime, you will have to weigh up how much longer the present social set-up can be maintained before considering such a move.

When thinking of emigration, most people think of the English-speaking countries, but there are now fewer obstacles to relocating to EC countries than there are to the more traditional destinations. Citizens of EC countries need no visas or work permits to work in other member states, and the main barrier to your working in the EC is likely to be your language ability rather than any regulations. Without some grasp of the language, you will be confined to unskilled work.

Whatever country attracts you as a potential relocation destination, it is advisable to visit the country before committing yourself to uprooting your home and family if you possibly can. If you are thinking of the EC countries, you can visit the EC for up to three months to look for a job and still claim your Unemployment Benefit. By visiting the country first, you can brush up on your language skill before taking a job. You can also make speculative applications to the government job-finding services of other EC countries. You will need to visit your jobcentre and to obtain form ES13 on which you set out your experience and qualifications. You will also need copies of your qualification certificates. The form is then forwarded to the country concerned and you will be informed if there are any suitable vacancies.

Leaving the Employment Market

If your occupation is so specialized that you will find it difficult to obtain a new job and you do not wish to retrain, or if you are approaching retirement age, you may wish to consider leaving the job market altogether. Few people are able to take this option, but below we describe some circumstances in which you may wish to consider this alternative.

Role Reversal

If you have a partner in full-time employment, whether you are male or female, you could consider allowing your partner's wage to support you. If you have children, the tax allowances and state benefits you will be able to claim could make the option of one of you not working an attractive one. Our society is still traditionally based and for a woman to make this decision is still much more acceptable than it is for a man. Now women are developing their careers, however, the situation will increasingly arise where the woman of a partnership earns more than the man. Couples who want children are going to have to make their own decisions about who stays at home to look after them in the early months or years, and in many situations it will be more logical for the husband to do so, possibly supplementing the family income with freelance, home-based work.

Early Retirement

If you have been offered early retirement by your employer, it may not be realistic to hope to re-enter the job market in full-time employment. You may wish to consider taking up part-time work or voluntary work as an alternative to full-time employment. Sit down and examine your finances carefully, and find out how much better off you would be from working full-time. If the answer is 'not a lot', think about whether you would prefer part-time work, perhaps self-employed part-time work. You could supplement your income with this and perhaps build up an entirely different second career. Many redundant executives take up consultancy work or you may have a hobby, such as furniture-making or dress-making, which could provide you with a part-time wage. You could consider temporary work rather than committing yourself full-time to another demanding job. Retired executives are much in demand by voluntary organizations who need their managerial expertise.

This chapter has given you some ideas which you can use either as alternatives to being unemployed or alternatives to conventional full-time employment. Redundancy is a breathing space on the treadmill of working life. Use it as such and think creatively about your situation. If you were happy with your previous occupation and lifestyle, then you will want to take up as quickly as possible from where you left off. If you were not happy, now is the time to think about steering your life in a more fulfilling direction. The next chapter will show you how to get the information on the alternatives we have discussed.

Chapter 9
Redundancy Information Guide

Benefits and Redundancy Guide

The Department of Social Security and the Department of Employment publish leaflets which cover almost every aspect of the benefits system. These leaflets are available from local Social Security Offices, from Unemployment Benefits Offices and from jobcentres. The leaflets are free and are well worth having. Those pertaining particularly to redundancy are produced by the Department of Employment, and the following may be useful:

Redundancy Payments (PL808)
Redundancy Consultation and Notification (PL833)
Facing Redundancy? – Time off for job hunting or to arrange training (PL703)
Employees' Rights on Insolvency of Employer (PL718)
Employment Rights on the Transfer of an Undertaking (PL699)
Unfairly Dismissed (PL712)

Jobcentres will usually have a good selection of brochures on training and re-employment programmes. These include:

Unemployed? How we can help you
Jobclubs
Restart Programmes

What's Due to You (Family Credit)
Job Interview Guarantee
How to be Better Off in Work
Employment Training

This list is by no means exhaustive.

Both the Department of Employment and the Department of Social Security operate helplines which are free to the caller, although the Social Security line is often engaged.

The Redundancy Helpline is   0800 848489
The Social Security Helpline is 0800 666555.

Useful Addresses

Employment Department Redundancy Payments Offices

Chesser House West
5th Floor
502 Gorgie Road
Edinburgh EH11 3YH
(031-443 8731)

Areas covered: Scotland and North-East England.

Ayton Street
Manchester M60 2HA
(061-236 4433)

Areas covered: North-West England.

2 Duchess Place
Hagley Road
Birmingham B16 8NS
(021-456 1144)

Areas covered: Midlands, Wales, East Anglia and South-West England.

Arena House
North End Road
Wembley HA9 0NF
(081-900 1966)

Areas covered: London and the South-East.

Industrial Tribunals
For England and
Wales:

Central Office of the Industrial Tribunals
93 Ebury Bridge Road
London SW1W 8RE

For Scotland: St Andrews House
                       141 West Nile Street
                       Glasgow G1 2RH

Citizens Advice Bureaux are listed in the telephone
directory under that heading.
Local branches of the **Child Poverty Action Group** are
similarly listed.

Job Finding

Agencies and Consultancies
The addresses and telephone numbers of these can be
found in your local *Yellow Pages* under the heading
'Employment Agencies'. Recruitment consultancies dealing
with managerial jobs tend to be based in large cities,
especially London. Some of the better known include:

AGB Human Resource   Specialization: General.
  Consultants
173-6 Sloane Street
Knightsbridge
London SW1X 9QB
(071-235 9891)

Alexander Hughes and   Specialization: General.
  Associates
Brummel House
33-9 Saville Row
London W1X 1AG
(071-287 9565)

ASA International   Specialization: Finance,
63 George Street   accounting, computing,
Edinburgh EH2 2JE   hi-tech. Also has offices in
(031-226 6222)   Glasgow and Aberdeen.

ASB Recruitment Ltd   Specialization: Finance,
Corn Exchange Buildings   accounting. Also has offices
19 Brunswick Street   in Leeds and Manchester.
Liverpool L2 0PJ
(051-236 9373)

Boyden International Ltd   Specialization: General.
148 Buckingham Palace Road
London SW1W 9TR
(071-730 5292)

Cambridge Recruitment   Specialization:
  Consultants   Manufacturing, engineering.
11 King's Parade
Cambridge CB2 1SJ
(0223 311316)

CPC Computer Personnel   Specialization: Computing,
  Consultants Ltd   hi-tech.
18th Floor: Rotunda
New Street
Birmingham B2 4PA
(021-632 6848)

Cripps Sears & Associates   Specialization: General.
71 Kingsway
London WC2B 6ST
(071-404 5701)

Douglas Llambias   Specialization: Finance,
  Associates   accounting.
Cavendish House   Also has offices in
39 Waterloo Street   London and Manchester.
Birmingham B2 5PP
(021-233 4421)

Egon Zehnder International Specialization: General.
Devonshire House
Mayfair Place
London W1X 5PH
(071-493 3882)

Ernst & Young Search and   Specialization: General,
  Selection   finance, accounting.
21 Conduit Street
London W1R 9TB
(071-495 7808)

Eurosurvey (UK) Ltd
18 Great Marlborough St.
London W1V 1AF
(071-437 3611)

Specialization: General,
manufacturing, engineering.

Goddard Kay Rogers Ltd
38 St James's Square
London SW1Y 4JR
(071-930 5100)

Specialization: General.
Also has offices in
Leeds and Manchester.

Heidrick and Struggles
   International
100 Piccadilly
London W1V 9EN
(071-491 3124)

Specialization: General.

Hoggett Bowers PLC
Abbott House
1/2 Hanover Street
London W1R 9WB
(071-734 6852)

Specialization: General.

Jamieson Scott
7 Belgrave Road
London SW1V 1QB
(071-834 8533)

Specialization: General.

Korn/Ferry International
Pepys House
12 Buckingham Street
London WC2N 6DF
(071-930 4334)

Specialization: General.

KPMG Peat Marwick
   McLintock
70 Fleet Street
London EC4Y 1EU
(071-236 8000)

Specialization: General,
finance, accounting.

Mach Consulting Group
36-9 Waterfront Quay
Salford Quays
Manchester M5 2XW
(061-872 3676)

Specialization: General.

Michael Page Finance
Clarendon House
81 Mosley Street
Manchester M2 3LQ
(061-228 0396)

Specialization: Finance, accounting.
Also has offices in London, Birmingham, Bristol, Glasgow, Eton, Nottingham, Leeds.

Moxon Dolphin Kerby
  Western
Park House
High Street
Thornby
Bristol BS12 2AG
(0454 413655)

Specialization: General.

MSL International (UK) Ltd
32 Aybrook Street
London W1M 3JL
(071-487 5000)

Specialization: General.

Norman Broadbent
  International Ltd
65 Curzon Street
London W1Y 7PE
(071-629 9626)

Specialization: General.

PA Consulting Group
123 Buckingham Palace Rd
London SW1W 9SR
(071-730 9000)

Specialization: Finance, accounting, computing, hi-tech.

Price Waterhouse
  Management Consultants
Milton Gate
1 Moor Lane
London EC2Y 9PB
(071-939 3000)

Specialization: General, finance, accounting.

Robert Half
7th Floor Mancher House
Mander Centre
Wolverhampton WV1 3NB
(0902 27079)

Specialization: Finance, accounting. Also offices in Leeds, Bristol, Manchester, London, Birmingham, Southampton.

Russell Reynolds   Specialization: General.
  Associates
24 St James's Square
London SW1Y 4HZ
(071-839 7788)

Selection Thompson Ltd   Specialization: General.
14 Sandyford Place
Glasgow G3 7NB
(041-248 3666)

Spencer Stuart &   Specialization: General.
  Associates
16 Connaught Place
London W2 2ED
(071-493 1238)

Tyzack & Partners   Specialization: General.
10 Hallam Street   Also offices in Leeds and
London W1N 6DJ   Bristol.
(071-580 2924)

Whitehead Mann Ltd   Specialization: General.
44 Welbeck Street
London W1M 7HF
(071-935 8978)

Getting Help

Careers Counsellors

CEPEC, 67 Jermyn Street, London SW1 6NY   071-976 1520

Chusid Lander Ltd, 35-37 Fitzroy Street, London W1. 071-580 6771

Coutts Career Consultants, 25 Whitehall, London SW1. 071-839 2271

Pauline Hyde Associates, 20 Lincolns Inn Fields, London WC2A 3ED.   071-242 4875

Sanders & Sidney Ltd, Orion House, 5 Upper St Martins Lane, London WC2H 9EA.   071-413 0321

Vocational Guidance

Career Analysts, Career House, 90 Gloucester Place, London W1.   071-935 5452

IARC/Ashridge (Independent Assessment & Research Centre), 17 Portland Place, London W1N 3AF.   071-935 2373

Vocational Guidance Association, 7 Harley House, Upper Harley Street, London NW1.   071-935 2600

Other Useful Addresses

Jobcentres are listed in the telephone book under 'Employment Service'.

For further training and re-training opportunities you should contact your local **Training and Enterprise Council** (TEC). The addresses of these are:

Thames Valley Enterprise TEC 6th Floor Kingspoint, 120 Kings Road, *Reading* RG1 3BZ   0734 568156

Essex TEC Globe House, New Street, *Chelmsford* CM1 1UG 0245 358548

Hampshire TEC 25 Thackeray Mall, *Fareham* PO16 0PQ 0329 285921

South Thames TEC 200 Great Dover Street, London SE1 4YB   071-403 1990

Hertfordshire TEC New Barnes Mill, Cotton Mill Lane, *St Albans* AL1 2HA   0727 52313

Isle of Wight TEC Mill Court, Furrlongs, *Newport* PO30 2AA   0983 833818

Kent TEC 5th Floor, Mountbatten House, 28 Military Road, *Chatham* ME4 4JE   0634 844411

Milton Keynes & N Bucks TEC Old Market Halls, Creed Street, *Milton Keynes* MK12 5LY   0908 222555

Heart of England TEC 26/27 The Quadrant, Abingdon Science Park, Barton Lane, *Abingdon* OX14 3YS 0235 553249

Surrey TEC Technology House, 48/54 Goldsworth Road, *Woking* GU21 1LE   0483 728190

Sussex TEC Gresham House, 12/24 Station Road, *Crawley* RH10 1HT   0293 562922

AZTEC Manorgate House, 2 Manorgate Road, *Kingston upon Thames* KT2 7AL   081-547 3934

Central London TEC c/o Employment Department, 236 Grays Inn Road, *London* WC1X 8HL   071-837 3311

CILNTEC c/o Employment Department, 256 Grays Inn Road, *London* WC1X 8HL   071-837 3311

London East TEC Cityside House, 40 Adler Street, *London* E1 1EE   071-377 1866

North London TEC c/o Employment Department, 19/29 Woburn Place, *London* WC1 0LU   071-837 1288

North West London TEC c/o Employment Department, 19/29 Woburn Place, *London* WC1 0LU   071-837 1288

SOLOTEC 7 Elmfield Road, *Bromley* BR1 1LT   081-313 9232

West London TEC c/o Employment Department, 149 Hammersmith Road, *London* W14 0QT   071-602 7227

Avon TEC PO Box 164, St Lawrence House, 29/31 Broad Street, *Bristol* BS99 7HR   0272 277116

Devon & Cornwall TEC North Road, BR Station, *Plymouth* PL4 6AA   0752 671671

Dorset TEC 25 Oxford Road, *Bournemouth* BH8 8EY   0202 299284

Gloucestershire TEC Conway House, 33/35 Worcester Street, *Gloucester* GL1 3AJ   0452 24488

Somerset TEC Crescent House, 37 The Mount, *Taunton* TA1 3TT   0823 259121

Wiltshire TEC The Bora Building, Westlea Campus, Westlea Down, *Swindon* SN5 7EZ   0793 513644

Birmingham TEC 16th Floor, Metro House, 1 Hagley Road, *Birmingham* B16 8TG   021 456 1199

Central England TEC The Oakes, Clews Road, *Redditch* B98 7ST   0527 545415

Coventry & Warwickshire TEC Brandon Court, Progress Way, *Coventry* CV3 2TE   0203 635666

Dudley TEC 5th Floor, Falcon House, The Minories, *Dudley* DY2 8PG   0384 455391

HAWTEC Hazwell House, St Nicholas Street, *Worcester* WR1 1UW   0905 26486

Sandwell TEC 1st Floor, Kingston House, 438/450 High Street, *West Bromwich* B70 9LD   021 525 4242

Shropshire TEC 2nd Floor, Hazeldene House, Central Square, *Telford* TF3 4JJ   0952 291471

Staffordshire TEC Moorlands House, 24 Trinity Street, *Stoke on Trent* ST1 5LN   0782 202733

Walsall TEC 5th Floor, Townend House, Townend Square, *Walsall* WS1 1NS   0922 32332

Wolverhampton TEC 2nd Floor, 30 Market Street, *Wolverhampton* WV1 3AF   0902 311111

Bedfordshire TEC Wolseley Business Park, Woburn Court Industrial Estate, *Kempton* MK42 7PN   0234 843100

CAMBSTEC Units 2/3 Trust Court, The Vision Park, *Cambridge* CB4 4PW   0223 235633

Greater Peterborough TEC Unit 4, Blenheim Court, Peppercorn Close, The Lincoln Road, *Peterborough* PE1 2DU   0733 890808

Leicestershire TEC Rutland Centre, Halford Street, *Leicester* LE1 1TQ   0533 538616

Lincolnshire TEC Wigford House, Brayford Wharf East, *Lincoln* LN5 7AY   0522 532266

Norfolk and Waveney TEC Partnership House, Unit 10 Norwich Business Park, Whiting Road, *Norwich* NR4 6DJ   0603 763812

Northamptonshire TEC c/o The Training Shop, 85/87 Weedon Road, *Northampton* NN5 5BG   0604 751175

North Derbyshire TEC Project Group, 58 Derby Road, *Chesterfield* S40 2ED   0246 551158

Greater Nottingham TEC Lambert House, Talbot Street, *Nottingham* NG1 5GL   0602 413313

North Nottinghamshire TEC 1st Floor, Block C Edwinstowe House, High Street, *Mansfield* NG21 9PR   0623 824624

Southern Derbyshire TEC St Peters House, Gower Street, *Derby* DE1 1SB   0332 290550

Suffolk TEC 2nd Floor, Crown House, Crown Street, *Ipswich* IP1 3HS   0473 218951

Barnsley/Doncaster TEC Conference Centre, Eldon Street, *Barnsley* S70 2TN   0226 248088

Bradford & District TEC 5th Floor, Provincial House, Tyrell Street, *Bradford* BD1 1NW   0274 723711

Calderdale & Kirklees TEC Park View House, Woodvale Road, *Brighouse* HD6 4AB   0484 400770

Humberside TEC The Maltings, Sylvester Square, *Hull* HU1 3HL   0482 226491

Leeds TEC Fairfax House, Merrion Street, *Leeds* LS2 8LH   0532 446181

North Yorkshire TEC 7 Pioneer Business Park, Amy Johnson Way, *York* YO3 8TN   0904 691939

Rotherham TEC Moorgate House, Moorgate Road, *Rotherham* S60 2EN   0709 830511

Sheffield TEC 1st Floor, Don House, 20/22 Hawley Street, *Sheffield* S1 3GA   0742 701911

Wakefield TEC York House, 31/36 York Place, *Leeds* LS1 2EB   0532 450502

Bolton/Bury TEC Bayley House, St George's Square, *Bolton* BL1 2HB   0204 397350

CEWTEC (Chester Ellesmere Port & Wirral TEC) Block 4, Woodside Business Park, *Birkenhead* L41 1EH   051 650 0555

Cumbria TEC Venture House, Regents Court, Guard Street, *Workington* CA14 4EW   0900 66991

ELTEC (East Lancashire TEC Ltd) Suite 506, Glenfield Park Site 2, Northrop Avenue, *Blackburn* BB1 5QF   0254 61471

LAWTEC (Lancashire West TEC) 4th Floor, Duchy House, 96 Lancaster Road, *Preston* PR1 1HE   0772 59393

Manchester TEC Boulton House, 17/21 Chorlton Street, *Manchester* M1 3HY   061 236 7222

Merseyside TEC c/o Employment Department, Tithebarn Street, *Liverpool* L2 2NZ   051 236 0026

NorMidTEC (North & Mid Cheshire TEC), c/o Employment Department, Spencer House, Dewhurst Road, *Warrington* WA3 7PP   0925 826515

Oldham TEC 3rd Floor, Block D, Brunswick Square, Union Street, *Oldham* OL1 1DE   061 620 0006

Rochdale TEC 160/162 Yorkshire Street, *Rochdale* OL16 2DL   0706 44909

South & East Cheshire TEC PO Box 37, Dalton Way, *Middlewich* CW10 0HU   0606 847009

QUALITEC (St Helens) Ltd, PO Box 113, St Helens, *Merseyside* WA10 3LN   0744 696300

Stockport/High Peak TEC 1 St Peters Square, *Stockport* SK1 1NN   061 477 8830

METROTEC (Wigan) Ltd, Buckingham Row, Northway, *Wigan* WN1 1XX   0942 36312

County Durham TEC Valley Street North, *Darlington* DL1 1TJ   0325 351166

Northumberland TEC Suite 2, Craster Court, Manor Walk, Shopping Centre, *Cramlington* NE23 6XX   0670 713303

Teesside TEC Corporation House, 73 Albert Road, *Middlesbrough* TS1 2RU   0642 231023

Tyneside TEC Moongate House, Team Valley Trading Estate, *Gateshead* NE11 0HF   091 487 5599

Wearside TEC Derwent House, New Town Centre, *Washington* NE38 7ST   091 416 6161

Gwent TEC Government Buildings, Cardiff Road, *Newport* NP9 1YE   0633 817777

Mid Glamorgan TEC Unit 17/20 Centre Court, Main Ave, Treforest Industrial Estate, *Pontypridd* CF37 5YL   0443 841594

North East Wales TEC Wynnstay Block, Kingsmill Road, *Wrexham* LL13 8BH   0978 290049

North West Wales TEC 1st Floor, Bron Castell, High Street, *Bangor* LL57 1YS   0248 370291

Powys TEC 1st Floor, St David's House, *Newtown* SY16 1RB   0686 622494

South Glamorgan TEC 5th Floor, Phase 1 Building, Ty Glas Road, Llanishen, *Cardiff* CF4 5PJ   0222 755744

West Wales TEC Orchard House, Orchard Street, *Swansea* SA1 5DJ   0792 460355

Enterprise Ayrshire Glencairn Business Centre, Low Glencairn Street, *Kilmarnock* KA1 4AY   0563 26623

Scottish Borders Enterprise c/o SDA Wheatlands Road, *Galashiels* TD1 2HQ   0896 58991

Dumfries & Galloway Enterprise Company c/o SDA, 16 Buccleuch Street, *Dumfries* DG1 2AH   0387 54444

Dunbartonshire Enterprise 2nd Floor, Spectrum House, Clydebank Business Park, *Clydebank* G81   041 951 2121

Fife Enterprise Huntsman House, 33 Cadham Centre, *Glenrothes* KY7 6RU   0592 754343

Forth Valley Enterprise Company c/o SDA, Alpha Centre, Stirling University Innovation Park, *Stirling* FK9 4NF   0786 70080

Glasgow Development Agency c/o SDA, 120 Bothwell Street, *Glasgow* G2 7JP   041 248 2700

Grampian Enterprise Ltd c/o SDA, 10 Queens Road, *Aberdeen* AB1 6YT   0224 641791

Lanarkshire Development Agency c/o SDA, 21 Bothwell Street, *Glasgow* G2 6NR   041 248 2700

Lothian and Edinburgh Enterprise Ltd c/o SDA, Rosebery House, Haymarket Terrace, *Edinburgh* EH12 5EZ   031 337 9595

Moray Badenoch & Strathspey Enterprise c/o HIDB, The Square, Granton on Spey, *Moray* PH26 3HF   0479 3288

Renfrewshire Enterprise Company c/o SDA, Marlin House, Mossland Road, Hillington, *Glasgow* G52 4XZ   041 882 6288

Scottish Enterprise Tayside Argyll House, Marketgait, *Dundee* DD1 1QP   0382 23100

Similarly you may find it useful to contact your local **welfare rights** or **unemployed centre**:

Grampian Welfare Rights, 47 Belmont Street, *Aberdeen* AB1 1JS   0224-648247

Aberdeen Unemployed Centre, 54 Frederick Street, *Aberdeen* AB2 1HY   0224-640113

Social Work Department, Strathclyde Regional Council, Adam Avenue, *Airdrie* ML6 6DN

Cogwheels Unemployed Centre, 19 Mar Street, *Alloa* FK10 1HR

Unemployed Centre, Unit 8J Industrial Estate, Easter Ross, *Alness* IV17   0349-884435

Ashington Unemployed Centre, Community Initiatives Centre, Kenilworth Road, *Ashington* NE63 8AA 0670-853619

Welfare Benefits Advice Service, Thameside MBC, Room 1-34 Council Offices, Wellington Road, *Ashton Under Lyne* OL6 6DL

Ayr Unemployed Centre, 61 Main Street, *Ayr* KA8 1BU 0292-286785

Barrow Unemployed Centre, 18 Vengeance Street, Walney, *Barrow-in-Furness* LA13

Bradford Centre Against Unemployment, 108 Sunbridge Road, *Bradford* BD1 2NE   02744-723304

Brighton Unemployed Centre, Tilbury Place, *Brighton* BN2 2GY

Burnley Unemployed Centre, 162 St. James Street, *Burnley* BB11 1NR

Bacup Unemployed Centre, 37 Todmorden Road, *Bacup* OL13 9EG

The Information Centre, Greenhouse, 1 Trevelyan Terrace, *Bangor* LL57 1AX

Bangor Unemployed Centre, 133 High Street, *Bangor* LL57 1NT

Bargoed Unemployed Activity Centre, Aeron Place, Gilbach,*Bargoed*

Barnsley Enterprise Centre, CEAG Building, 1 Pontefract Road, *Barnsley* S71 1AJ

Barrhead & Neilston Unemployed Centre, Calibar Primary School, Main Street, *Barrhead* G78

Vale CMHT (Welfare Rights Worker), 26 Newlands Street, *Barry* CF6 6EA

Basildon Council Welfare Rights Office, Bryn Centre, Church Road, *Basildon* SS14 2EX

'Open Door', Market Chambers, Church Street, *Basingstoke*

Regal Resource Centre for the Unemployed, 24-34 North Bridge Street, *Bathgate* EH48 4PS   0506-630017

North Kirklees CVS, 13 Hanover Street, *Batley* WF17 5DZ   00924 472702

Bedford Unemployed Centre, 125A High Street, *Bedford* MK40 1NU   0234-64558

Belfast Unemployed Centre, 45 Donegall Street, *Belfast* BT1 2FG

Bexley Centre for the Unemployed, Trinity Place, Broadway, *Bexleyheath* DA6 7AY

Cleveland Social Services, Municipal Buildings, Town Centre, *Billingham* TS23

Welfare Benefits Advice Unit, Wirral Social Services Centre, Cleveland Street, *Birkenhead* L41 6BL

West Midlands Welfare Rights Agency, 3rd Floor, Spencer House, Digbeth, *Birmingham* B5 6DD 021-622-7446

Tyseley Training & Community Resource Centre, 124 Amington Road, Tyseley, *Birmingham* B25 8EP

Chelmsley Advice & Resource Centre, Keeper's Lodge, Chelmsley Road, *Birmingham* B37 7RS 021-770-3773

Birmingham Trades Council Unemployed Centre, 448 Stratford Road, Sparkhill, *Birmingham* B11 4AE 021-771-0871

Blyth Unemployed Centre, 22-26 Bowed Street, *Blyth* NE24

Bolton Unemployed Workers Centre, 16 Wood Street, *Bolton* BL1 1DY

City Centre Project, 1st Floor, Patrick Centre, Sedgefield, *Bradford* BD1

Bradford Resource Centre, 31 Manor Row, *Bradford* BD1 4PS

Braintree Unemployed Centre, The Annexe, Town Hall, *Braintree* CM7

Brampton Unemployed Drop In Centre, Union Lane, *Brampton* CA8

Welfare Benefits, Social Services Department, Mid Glamorgan County Council, Sunnyside, *Bridgend* CF31 4AR

Bridgend Unemployed Centre, Blaengarw Activity Centre, Church Place, Blaengarw, *Bridgend* CF31

Brighton Rights Advice Centre, 102a North Road, *Brighton* BN1 1YE

Brighton Unemployed Centre, Tilbury Place, *Brighton* BN2 2GY 0273-671213

St Paul's Advice Centre, 146 Grosvenor Road, *Bristol* BS2 8YA

Bury Centre for the Unemployed, 12 Tithebarn Street, *Bury* BL9 0JR

Bury St Edmunds Unemployed Centre, Lansbury House, Crown Street, *Bury St. Edmunds* IP33 1SN

Caldicot Community Enterprise Resource, Old Post Office, 5A Church Road, *Caldicot*

Cambridge Benefits Advice Centre, 102 Regent Street, *Cambridge* CB2 1DP   0223-353617

Cambuslang Unemployed Centre, Morriston Street, *Cambuslang* G72 7HZ   041-641-5434

Benefits Advice Centre, 5 Old Post Office Court, *Carlisle* CA3 8LE

Chester Unemployed Centre, George Street, *Chester* CH1 3HX

Chesterfield Unemployed Centre, 54 Saltergate, *Chesterfield* S40 1JR

Chorley Unemployment Group (CHUG), Unit 1 Hollinshead Street, *Chorley* PR7 1EP

Corby Unemployed Activity Centre, Epiphany Church Hall, Elizabeth Street, *Corby*

Coventry Unemployed Workers Project, Unit 15, The Arches Industrial Estate, Spon End, *Coventry* CV1 3JQ   0203-714082

Rights Office Fife, 30-32 High Street, *Cowdenbeath* KY4 9NA   0383-515245

Crawley Community Resources Centre, 17 Spencers Road, *Crawley* RH11 7DE

Croydon Unemployed Resource Centre, 70a Wellesley Road, *Croydon* CR0 2AR

Cumbernauld Unemployed Centre, Town Centre South, *Cumbernauld* G67 1XX

Dalkeith Unemployed Centre, 10 Woodburn Road, *Dalkeith* EH22 2AR   031-663-0400

Darlington Unemployed Centre, Old Town Hall, Horsemarket, *Darlington* DL1 5PU

Sinfin Unemployment Project, 60 Shakespeare Street, *Derby* DE2 9HE

Derby Unemployed Centre, Woods Lane, Centre 31 Woods Lane, *Derby* DE1

Kirklees Directorate of Social Services, Victoria Centre, Wellington Road, *Dewsbury* WF13 1HN

Doncaster Unemployed Centre, Wood Street, *Doncaster* DN1 3LN

Dumfries Unemployed Centre, 29 Irish Street, *Dumfries* DG1 2PJ

Dundee Resource Centre for the Unemployed, 61 Reform Street, *Dundee* DD3 1SP   0382-27735

Fife Unemployed Centre, Fife Rights Office, 12 Viewfield Terrace, *Dunfermline* KY12 7HZ   0383-732320

Durham County Council Welfare Rights Unit, County Hall, *Durham* DH1 5UG

East Kilbride Unemployed Centre, Murray Hall, Rotunda, *East Kilbride* G75   041-32-46520

Benefits Unit, Barnet Borough Council, Barnard House, 158 Burnt Oak, Broadway, *Edgeware* HA8 0UH

Citizens Rights Office, 43 Broughton Street, *Edinburgh* EH1 3JU

NETWORK Tenant & Worker Information, Ainslie House, 11 St. Colme Street, *Edinburgh* EH3 6AG   031-225-4606

Southbridge Resource Centre, Southbridge School, Infirmary Street, *Edinburgh* EH1

Edinburgh Unemployed Workers Centre, 103 Broughton Street, *Edinburgh* EH1 3RZ   031-557-0718

Moray Unemployed & Welfare Rights Advice Centre, Trinity Road, *Elgin* IV30 1UE   0343-48226

King Street, Unemployed & Resource Centre, King Street, *Ellesmere Port* L65 4AZ

LB Enfield Social Services Department, 3 Pitfield Way, *Enfield* EN3 5QX   081-805-2366

Central Money Advice Project, 3/5 Chapel Lane, *Falkirk* FK1 5BB

Falkirk Unemployed Advisory Service, Bean Row (Off Cow Wynd), *Falkirk*

Folkestone Unemployed Centre, Bouverie Chambers, Bouverie Square, *Folkestone* CT20 1BD

Resource Centre 'One Plus', 39 Hope Street, *Glasgow* G2 6AE

Temple Shafton Youth Project, Community Flat, 2 Shafton Road, 2-4 *Glasgow* G13 2NB   041-954-6541

Glasgow Federation of Unemployed Centres, District Trades Council, 83 Carlton Place, *Glasgow* G5 041-429-4845

Govan Unemployed Centre, Rathlin Street, Govan, *Glasgow* G51 3AG   041-445-4263

Drumchapel Unemployed Centre, 5 Hecla Place, Drumchapel, *Glasgow* G13 041-944-9400

East End Community Resource Centre, St Mungo's Academy, Crownpoint Road, *Glasgow* G40 2RA

Garthamlock Unemployed Workers Centre, c/o Woodcroft School, 7 Findochty Street, *Glasgow* G33 5EQ 041-774-6884

Gorbals Unemployed Centre, Waddell Street, Gorbals, *Glasgow*

Ruchill Unemployed Centre, 201 Shuna Hill, Ruchill, *Glasgow*

Johnstone Unemployed Centre, Drill Hall, Dimity Street, Johnstone, *Glasgow*

Milton Unemployed Centre, 460 Ashgill Road, Milton, *Glasgow* G22

Anderston Unemployed Centre, Port Street, Anderston, *Glasgow* G3 8HY

Dougrie Unemployed Centre, Dougrie Terrace, Castlemilk, *Glasgow* G45

Laurieston Information Centre, 80 Stirlingfauld Place, *Glasgow* G5 9BS 041-429-3245

Rights Office Fife, 11 Hanover Court, North Street, *Glenrothes* KY7 5SB 0592-758969

Guildford Area Unemployed Centre, 3a Leapale Road, *Guildford* GU1 4JX

Hamilton Unemployed Centre, Hamilton Centre for Information, Leechlee Road, *Hamilton* ML3 6AW

Harlow Trade Union & Unemployed Resource Centre, 2 Wych Elm, *Harlow* CM20 1QP 0279-435000

Focus 230, 230 Dunsbury Way, Leigh Park, *Havant* PO9

Hebburn Neighbourhood Advice Centre, 9a Station Road, *Hebburn* NE31 1NX

Holyhead Unemployed Centre, Townrow House, Hill Street, *Holyhead* LL65 1NE

Workers Support Unit & Centre for the Unemployed, 18 Staines Road, *Hounslow* TW3 1JG 081-572 3764

The Warren Centre, 47-49 Queens Dock Avenue, Queens Gardens, *Hull* HU1 3DR 0482-218115

Hull Unemployed Centre, 16 Hannover Square, c/o Guildhall, *Hull* HU1

Ipswich Unemployed Centre, 16 Old Foundry Road, *Ipswich* IP4 2DU

Irvine Unemployed Centre, 17 Townhead, *Irvine* KA12 0294-71716

Jarrow Unemployed Centre, 1st Floor, Civic Hall, Ellison Street, *Jarrow*

Welfare Rights Advisory Service, 15 London Road, *Kettering* NN16 0EF

Yack Advice Line, William Knibb Centre, Montagu Street, *Kettering* NN16 8AE 520089

Shortlees & Riccarton Advice Service, Community Flat, 42-48 Barnwell Road, *Kilmarnock* KA1 4JF

Unemployment Project, St Joseph's Academy, Grassyards Road, *Kilmarnock* KA3 7SL

Kirby Unemployed Centre, Westhead Avenue, Northwood, *Kirby* L33 0XN 051-548-0001

Rights Office Fife, 10 East Fergus Place, *Kirkcaldy* KY1 1XT 0592-205556

Unemployed Centre, YMCA, China Street, *Lancaster* LA1 1EX

Braunstone Employment Project, 9 Cantrell Road, Braunstone, *Leicester* LE3 1SD 892186

Belle Vue Resource Unit, Belle Vue Centre, Belle Vue Road, *Leeds* LS3 1HG

Leeds Unemployed & Claimants Union, 158 Hyde Park Road, *Leeds* LS6 1AG

'95' Family Service Unit, 95 Hand Avenue, *Leicester* LE3 1SN 0533-858009

Leicester Rights Centre, 6 Bishops Street, *Leicester* LE1 6AF

Money Advice Unit, 10 Granby Street, *Leicester* LE1 1DE 0533-627761

Project Vbx, 4a Main Street, Newold Verdon, *Leicester* LE9 9NL

Leicester Unemployed Centre, 138 Charles Street, *Leicester* LE1 1LB

Merseyside Welfare Rights, 24 Hardman Street, (Ground Floor), *Liverpool* L1 9AX 051-709-0504

Merseyside TU & Unemployed Centre, 24 Hardman Street, *Liverpool* L1 9AX 051-709-3995

Knowsley Stockbridge Resource Centre, Nine Trees CP School, Hollowcraft, Cantril Farm, *Liverpool* L28 051-489-4841

Huyton Unemployed Centre, Lathom Road, Huyton, *Liverpool* L36

Piccadilly Advice Centre, 100 Shaftesbury Avenue, *London* W1V 7DH

Lambeth Welfare Rights Unit, 138-146 Clapham Park Road, *London* SW4 7DD   071-622-6655

Camden Welfare Rights Unit, LB Camden, Town Hall Extension, Euston Road, *London* NW1 2RU

Islington Welfare Rights Officer, Town Hall, Upper Street, *London* N1 2UD

Islington Peoples Rights, 2 St Pauls Road, *London* N1

Pluto Advice Centre, Old Laundry, Montem School, Hornsey Road, *London* N7 7QT   071-281-2121

Hackney Trade Union Support Unit, Liberty Hall, 489 Kingsland Road, *London* E8 4AU

Hackney Welfare Rights Unit, 136-142 Lower Clapton Road, *London* E5 0QJ

Greenwich Welfare Rights Unit, 8th Floor, Riverside House, Beresford Street, *London* SE18 6PW

Wandsworth Welfare Rights Unit, Balham Social Services, 114 Balham High Road, *London* SW12 9AA   071-871-6221

Newham Welfare Rights Team, 99 The Grove (Rooms 310-311), Stratford, *London* E15 1HR   081-534-4545

London Borough of Ealing Welfare Rights Unit, 3rd Floor, Percival House, 14-16 Uxbridge Road, *London* W5 2HL

Ethnic Advice And Community Service, 7 Chicksand Street (1st Floor), *London* E1 5LD

SCVS Employment Unit, 135 Rye Lane, *London* SE15

Community Affairs Unit, Lewisham Town Hall, Catford *London* SE6

Lambeth Social Services, 91 Clapham High Street, *London* SW4

Local Employment Advice Project, Bishop Creighton House, 378 Lillie Road, *London* SW6 7PU

Resource Centre, 9 Thorpe Close, *London* W10 5XL

Shepherds Bush Outreach Project, 1 Stowe Road, *London* W12 8TB

City of Westminster Social Services, 155 Westbourne Terrace, *London* W2 6JX 071-798-1424

Hammersmith Unemployed Centre, 190 Shepherds Bush Road, *London* W6 7NL 071-603-4278

Waltham Forest TURC, Markhouse Road School Complex, Markhouse Road, *London* E17 8BD 081-509-2243

Catford Unemployed Centre, 20 Holbeach Road, Catford, *London* SE6 4QX 081-690-8427

North Kensington Unemployed Centre, Wornington Road, *London* W10

Lambeth TUC Unemployed Workers Centre, 12-14 Thornton Street, *London* SW9 0BL 071-733-5135

Haringey Unemployed Centre, 30 Church Road, *London* N17 9CT 081-801-5629

Mary Ward Unemployed & Unwaged Group, Mary Ward Centre, 42 Queens Square, *London* WC1

Luton TUC Unemployed Centre, 13 Guildford Street, *Luton* LU2 2NQ 0582-453372

RAFT Centre for the Unemployed, Cottage Street, *Macclesfield*

Shades City Centre Project, 48 Copperas Street, *Manchester* M4 1HS

Welfare Rights Service, Marton House, Borough Road, *Middlesbrough* TS4 2EH 0642-248155

Milton Keynes Welfare Rights Group, 6 Church Street, Wolverton, *Milton Keynes* MK12 5UN

Musselburgh Unemployed Centre, Court Suite, Brunton Hall, *Musselburgh* EH21 031-665-8858

Newcastle TUC Centre Against Unemployment, 4 The Cloth Market, *Newcastle upon Tyne* NE1 091-232-4606

Northampton Unemployed Centre, 3-7 Hazelwood Road, *Northampton* NN1 1LG

Actionline, 48 St Giles Street, *Norwich* NR2 1LP 0603-611192

Unemployed Centre, Dukeries Complex, Whinney Lane, New Ollerton, *Newark* NG22 9TD 0623-8622363

Rights Office Fife, 65a High Street, *Newburgh* KY14 6AH 0337-40988

Newport Resource Centre, 35 Commercial Road, *Newport* NP9 2PB

North Tyneside Advice & Information Service, 60 Bedford Street, *North Shields* NE29 0AL

Welfare Rights Support Unit, 13 Hazelwood Road, *Northampton* NN1 1LG

Norwich Unemployed & Claimants Union, St Ann's Cottage, St Ann Lane, King Street, *Norwich* NR1 1QG   0603-661241

Family First, 32 Waterloo Road, *Nottingham* NG7 4AU   0602-788312

Oldham Welfare Rights, Metropolitan House, Hobson Street, *Oldham* OL1 1UY   061-624-0505

Oxford Unemployed Workers & Claimants Union, 44b Princes Street, *Oxford* OX4 1DD

'Step One', 70 Broadway, *Peterborough* PE1 1SU   0733-310107

Paisley Unemployed Workers Centre, 71 George Street, *Paisley* PA1 2JY   041-887-8118

Prescot Unemployed Centre, Council Buildings (Rear), High Street, *Prescot* L34   051-426-8262

Preston Unemployed Resource Centre, 'Open House', 3-5 Grimshaw Street, *Preston* PR1 3DD   0772-201690

R.E.D.I., 54 South Street, *Redditch* B98 7DQ

Retford Action Centre, 24a The Square, *Retford* DN22 6DQ   476118

Derbyshire Social Services, Cemetery Lane, *Ripley* DE5 3HY   0773-46101

Dearne Centre Against Unemployment, Dearne Enterprise Centre, 1 Barnburgh Lane, *Rotherham* S63 9PG Roth-897703

Halton CVS (Welfare Rights Co-ordinator), Brook Chambers, High Street, *Runcorn* WA7 1JH   0928-577626

Runcorn Unemployed Resource Centre, 5 King Street, *Runcorn* WA7

CATCH Centre for Young Unemployed, 209 Seneschal Square, Southgate, *Runcorn* WA7

Rutherglen Unemployed Centre, Victoria Street, *Rutherglen* G73   041-647-0331

Salford Unemployed Centre, 84-86 Liverpool Road, Eccles, *Salford* M30 0WB

Three Towns Unemployed Centre, 18-20 Countess Street, *Saltcoats*, Ayrshire

Sandwell Unwaged Resources Initiative, 434 St Marks Road, *Tipton* DY4 0SZ

Sandwell Community Development Officer, Department of Social Services, 12 Lombard Street, *Sandwell* B70 8RT 021-569-5455

Sheerness Unemployed Centre, 305 Richmond Street, Marine Town, *Sheerness* ME12 2QD

Sheffield Co-ordinating Centre Against Unemployment, 73 West Street, *Sheffield* S1 4EQ 0742-724866

Slough Unemployed Centre, 29 Church Street, *Slough* SL1 1PL

Welfare Rights Service, South Tyneside MBC, 1 Ferry Street, *South Shields* NE33 1JP

Unemployed Activities Centre, Gresford Road, *South Shields* NE33

Southampton Unemployed Centre, 11 Porchester Road, Woolston, *Southampton* SO2 7TB

St Helens Advice Guidance Service, 95 Corporation Street, *St Helens* WA10 1PZ

Stevenage Unemployed Centre, 4th Floor, Daneshill House, Danestrete, *Stevenage* SG1 1HN

Stirling District Council Community Resource Centre, 13 Corn Exchange Road, *Stirling* FK8 2HX 0786-79000

Off The Record, 67 Murray Place, PO Box 53, *Stirling* FK8 1YE 0786-505189

Welfare Rights Unit, Stockport MBC, Old Rectory, Churchgate, *Stockport* SK1 1YG 061-480-4949

Lewis Unemployed Centre, YMCA Bayhead, *Stornoway* PA87 2DU

S.N.A.P., Old Town Hall, 273 Southwick Road, *Sunderland* SR5 2AB

Sunderland TUC Unemployed Centre, 19 Foyle Street, *Sunderland* SR1 1LE

WEA Unemployed Centre, 37a Regent Street, *Swindon*

Thornaby Unemployed Centre, Thornaby Town Hall, Mandale Road, *Thornaby on Tees*

Ushington Resource Centre, Haldane Street, *Ushington* NE63 0SF

Wakefield Unemployed Centre, 25 King Street, *Wakefield* WF1 2SR   0924-295949

Wallasey Unemployed Centre, 108 Seaview Road, *Wallasey* L45

Wallsend People's Centre, 67 Charlotte Street, *Wallsend* NE28 7PU   091-263-5029

Unemployed Workers Centre, Silver Street, South Orford, *Warrington*

Watford Centre for the Unemployed, Central Library, *Watford* WD1 3EV

Brent Welfare Rights Unit, Room 5, Town Hall Annexe, Forty Lane, *Wembley* HA9 9HX

Sandwell Unemployed Centre, 324 High Street, *West Bromwich* B70 8DT

Wigan Unemployed Centre, 11 New Market Street, *Wigan* WN1 1SE

Bebington Unemployed Centre, 101 New Chester Road, Bebington, *Wirral* L62 4RA

Welfare Rights Office, Wolverhampton Social Services Department, 19 Victoria Street, *Wolverhampton* WV1 3NP

Bushbury Unemployed Group Unit, 25-26 Steel Drive, Fordhouse Road, Bushbury, *Wolverhampton*

B.R.A.G., King Street, Bradley, *Wolverhampton* WV14 9HL

C.H.E.E.R.S., Trades Hall, 39 Brow Top, *Workington* CA14 5DP   0900-61874

Bassetlaw Employment and Benefit Advice Centre, Church Walk, *Worksop* S80 2EJ

Worthing Unemployed Centre, Corporation House, High Street, *Worthing* BN11 1DJ   0903-31011

Clwyd Unemployed Centre, 4 Caernarvon Terrace, Clarke Street, Ponciau, *Wrexham*

North Yorkshire Welfare Benefits Unit, 8 The Crescent, Blossom Street, *York* YO2 2AW

Further Information and Reading

As you get into your job search there are many books that you may want to read. We give some that you may find of interest below:

Career Change, Ruth Lancashire and Roger Holdsworth, Hobsons Press, Cambridge, 1987

Manage Your Own Career: A Self-help Guide to Career Choice and Change, Ben Ball, The British Psychological Society, 1989

Managing Your Own Career, Dave Francis, Fontana, 1985

Smart Moves, Godfrey Golzen and Andrew Garner, Blackwell Press, 1990

The Daily Telegraph Recruitment Handbook, Patricia Leighton, Kogan Page, 1990

The Unemployment Handbook, Guy Dauncey, National Extension College, Cambridge, 1987

Build Your Own Rainbow, Hobson and Scally, Lifeskills Associates

What Colour is Your Parachute? Richard Bolles, Ten Speed Press, 1983

Jobkey, Newpoint Publishing Company Ltd, London

Occupations, Careers and Occupational Information Centre, Sheffield. Published annually, covering opportunities in the professions, industry, commerce and the public service.

Coping with Interviews, Martin Higham, Newpoint Publishing Company Ltd, 1987

How to be Interviewed, D. Mackenzie Davey and P. McDonnell, British Institute of Management, London, 1983

Croners Reference Book for the Self-employed, Croner Publications Ltd, New Malden, Surrey

Earning Money at Home, Edith Rudinger (ed.), Consumers' Association, 1988

Going Freelance, Godfrey Golzen, Kogan Page, 1989

The Guardian Guide to Running a Small Business, Kogan Page, 1988

The Pitfalls of Managing a Small Business, and How to Avoid Them, Dun and Bradstreet. Free from the publishers, tel. 071-377 4377.

Starting a Business on a Shoestring, Michel Syrett and Chris
  Dunn, Penguin, 1988
Unemployment and Training Rights Handbook, Dan Finn and
  Lucy Ball, The Independent Unemployment Unit, 1991

If you should opt for any form of self-employment the
following information may also be useful:

Enterprise Allowance Scheme
This is a nationwide scheme to help people to start their
own businesses. A £40 taxable weekly allowance is
available for one year to assist unemployed people to start
in business. The allowance is available to people meeting
all the following conditions:

- Are in receipt of unemployment benefit or
  supplementary benefit
- Have been unemployed or under personal notice of
  redundancy for at least 8 weeks
- Are over 18 and under statutory retirement age
- Have £1,000 available to invest in the business
- Will work full-time in the business
- Propose to set up a small business which is new,
  independent and suitable for public funding.

To apply for this scheme contact your local jobcentre who
will provide further details. If you appear to be eligible you
can then attend an information session where application
forms will be distributed. There are compulsory training
seminars called 'Awareness Days' which applicants must
attend. You must not start your business before your
application for the allowance has been approved.

Information sources include:

Alliance of Small Firms and Self-employed People, 33 The
Green, Calne, Wilts, SN11 8DJ

Association of British Chambers of Commerce, Sovereign
House, 212a Shaftesbury Avenue, London WC2H 8EW

Association of Independent Businesses, Trowbray House,
108 Weston Street, London SE1 3QB

British Franchise Association, Franchise Chambers, Thames View, Newtown Road, Henley-on-Thames, Oxon RG9 1HG

Enterprise Agencies
There are numerous local enterprise agencies and enterprise trusts throughout the UK. They will give independent advice and counselling on starting up in business.
Other useful sources of further information and assistance are:
Institute of Small Businesses, 14 Willow Street, London EC2A 4BH. Provide confidential business appraisal service; information advisory service.
Investors in Industry plc, 91 Waterloo Road, London SE1 8XP
London Enterprise Agency, 4 Snow Hill, London EC1A 2BS. Acts as a go-between for individuals or companies with resources and skills to offer.
National Federation of Self-employed and Small Businesses, 32 St Annes Road West, Lytham St Annes, Lancashire FY8 1NY
The Rural Development Commission. Their head office is at: 141 Castle Street, Salisbury, Wilts. The Commission's role in Scotland and Wales is undertaken respectively by:
The Scottish Development Agency, Rosebery House, Haymarket Terrace, Haymarket, Edinburgh EH12 5EZ
and
The Welsh Development Agency, Pearl House, Greyfriars Road, Cardiff CF1 3XX
Scottish Tourist Board, 23 Ravelston Terrace, Edinburgh EH2 3EU
Small Firms Service. Run by the Training Agency which is affiliated to the Department of Employment. Has 13 offices in England. Scotland and Wales are covered by the agencies listed above under 'Rural Development Commission'. Has basic start-up pack covering setting-up in business, accounting, marketing, finance, etc., and other useful booklets, eg. *Starting in Business, Raising Finance*. For your local office, dial 100 and ask the operator for Freefone Enterprise.
URBED (Urban Enterprise Development), 3 Stamford Street, London SE1 9NT

Afterword
Redundancy – Past, Present and Future

The system of redundancy payments which now operates was introduced into the legislation by the Redundancy Payments Act (1965). Strange though it may now seem, the Redundancy Payments Act was not introduced to make unemployment easier for those made redundant, but to alleviate a labour shortage. After the Second World War Britain's industrial growth had created a labour shortage which was seen as aggravated by management's reluctance to cause union trouble by shedding excess labour. New machinery and productivity practices meant that many companies did in fact have surplus labour and redundancy payments were seen as a way of making it easier for management to encourage workers to leave over-staffed companies and gravitate towards those suffering from labour shortage. This carrot approach was backed up by the stick of the Selective Employment Tax whereby employers in what were thought to be overmanned industries paid a tax based on the size of their workforce. Ray Gunter, then Minister of Labour presented the Redundancy Payments Act to Parliament as

An active policy to make it easier for workers to change . . . to ensure the planned use of resources especially our resources of manpower . . . an important component to our efforts to develop science-based industries and to deploy our manpower resources where they can make the most effective contriution to the economy. [Hansard 1965]

The consequences of the Redundancy Payments Act were to make it easier for 'good' employers to make redundancies and for redundancies to become more acceptable. Unfortunately the labour shortage which the Act was designed to alleviate was shortlived and the new jobs which it was envisaged would absorb redeployed labour failed to materialize at the anticipated rate. The latter half of the sixties was also marked by a change in government strategy with regard to employment policy. The spectre of 1930s unemployment had haunted post-War governments and government popularity was seen as dependent on maintaining full employment. As public memories of high unemployment faded, however, this relationship ceased to hold. Increasingly inflation took over public preoccupation as 'the problem' and govermnents found that they could maintain their popularity with the voters with what would once have seemed the unthinkable figure of *one million* unemployed.

As the redundant have found it more and more difficult to secure new jobs, larger companies have intervened in the labour market with various measures to try and find new employment for their ex-employees. These have included using the services of outplacement agencies and other more radical programmes. Rank Xerox has been providing facilities for redundant employees to set themselves up as freelance programmers working from home. GEC has instituted job sharing, particularly in order to provide job opportunities for younger people. British Steel has given financial and other help to companies setting up in areas where it is making large-scale redundancies. This trend, as with other trends in employee relations, will gradually spread from the larger companies to the smaller ones and employers are likely to find themselves increasingly involved in providing for the future of those employees they displace. The financial provision which has hitherto seemed satisfactory to employees will no longer be thought sufficient and employers will find themselves having to do more for their redundant staff.

Although the unemployment situation will stabilize and the rest of the 1980s and the 1990s will not see the same vast percentage increases in unemployment as did the 1970s and early 1980s, redundancy is likely to be an increasing part of people's lives. The increasing rate of industrial and commercial change will mean that old jobs and skills will become obsolete and people will be forced to retrain and to take up new jobs in the course of their careers. This may change the whole pattern of education, with higher and further education in particular, no longer being the province of the young. Workers will need to go into and out of education during their careers not only to learn new skills, but also to update their old skills. A one-off apprenticeship from age 16 to 20 will no longer launch someone into a job for life.

The increased likelihood of redundancy happening to people at least once in their working lives does not have to sound a note of doom and gloom. As employers recognize their responsibilities to ensure the future of their redundant employees, redundancy will come to be seen not as a threat but as a challenge and an opportunity. Redundancy is not something to be feared but is an opportunity to find a better job, to get better qualified, and to find out something about yourself. Don't fear redundancy but use it to build a better life for you and your family.

Ready Reckoner

Use this Ready Reckoner table for calculating the number of week's redundancy pay due to you:

- Read off your age and number of complete years' service. The table will then show how many weeks' pay you are entitled to. The table starts at 20 because no one below this age can qualify for a redundancy payment – service before the employee reached the age of 18 does not count.
- For employees aged between 64 and 65, the cash amount due is to be reduced by one twelfth for every complete month by which the age exceeds 64.

Service (years)

Age (years)	2	3	4	5	6	7	8	9	10	11	12	13	14	15	16	17	18	19	20
20	1	1	1	1	–														
21	1	1½	1½	1½	1½	–													
22	1	1½	2	2	2	2	–												
23	1½	2	2½	3	3	3	3	–											
24	2	2½	3	3½	4	4	4	4	–										
25	2	3	3½	4	4½	5	5	5	5	–									
26	2	3	4	4½	5	5½	6	6	6	6	–								
27	2	3	4	5	5½	6	6½	7	7	7	7	–							
28	2	3	4	5	6	6½	7	7½	8	8	8	8	–						
29	2	3	4	5	6	7	7½	8	8½	9	9	9	9	–					

Age (years)	2	3	4	5	6	7	8	9	10	11	12	13	14	15	16	17	18	19	20
30	2	3	4	5	6	7	8	8½	9	9½	10	10	10	10	-				
31	2	3	4	5	6	7	8	9	9½	10	10½	11	11	11	11	-			
32	2	3	4	5	6	7	8	9	10	10½	11	11½	12	12	12	12	-		
33	2	3	4	5	6	7	8	9	10	11	11½	12	12½	13	13	13	13	-	
34	2	3	4	5	6	7	8	9	10	11	12	12½	13	13½	14	14	14	14	-
35	2	3	4	5	6	7	8	9	10	11	12	13	13½	14	14½	15	15	15	15
36	2	3	4	5	6	7	8	9	10	11	12	13	14	14½	15	15½	16	16	16
37	2	3	4	5	6	7	8	9	10	11	12	13	14	15	15½	16	16½	17	17
38	2	3	4	5	6	7	8	9	10	11	12	13	14	15	16	16½	17	17½	18
39	2	3	4	5	6	7	8	9	10	11	12	13	14	15	16	17	17½	18	18½
40	2	3	4	5	6	7	8	9	10	11	12	13	14	15	16	17	18	18½	19
41	2	3	4	5	6	7	8	9	10	11	12	13	14	15	16	17	18	19	19½
42	2½	3½	4½	5½	6½	7½	8½	9½	10½	11½	12½	13½	14½	15½	16½	17½	18½	19½	20½
43	3	4	5	6	7	8	9	10	11	12	13	14	15	16	17	18	19	20	21
44	3½	4½	5½	6½	7½	8½	9½	10½	11½	12½	13½	14½	15½	16½	17½	18½	19½	20½	21½
45	3	4½	6	7	8	9	10	11	12	13	14	15	16	17	18	19	20	21	22
46	3	4½	6	7½	8½	9½	10½	11½	12½	13½	14½	15½	16½	17½	18½	19½	20½	21½	22½
47	3	4½	6	7½	9	10	11	12	13	14	15	16	17	18	19	20	21	22	23
48	3	4½	6	7½	9	10½	11½	12½	13½	14½	15½	16½	17½	18½	19½	20½	21½	22½	23½
49	3	4½	6	7½	9	10½	12	13	14	15	16	17	18	19	20	21	22	23	24
50	3	4½	6	7½	9	10½	12	13½	14½	15½	16½	17½	18½	19½	20½	21½	22½	23½	24½
51	3	4½	6	7½	9	10½	12	13½	15	16	17	18	19	20	21	22	23	24	25
52	3	4½	6	7½	9	10½	12	13½	15	16½	17½	18½	19½	20½	21½	22½	23½	24½	25½
53	3	4½	6	7½	9	10½	12	13½	15	16½	18	19	20	21	22	23	24	25	26
54	3	4½	6	7½	9	10½	12	13½	15	16½	18	19½	20½	21½	22½	23½	24½	25½	26½
55	3	4½	6	7½	9	10½	12	13½	15	16½	18	19½	21	22	23	24	25	26	27
56	3	4½	6	7½	9	10½	12	13½	15	16½	18	19½	21	22½	23½	24½	25½	26½	27½
57	3	4½	6	7½	9	10½	12	13½	15	16½	18	19½	21	22½	24	25	26	27	28
58	3	4½	6	7½	9	10½	12	13½	15	16½	18	19½	21	22½	24	25½	26½	27½	28½
59	3	4½	6	7½	9	10½	12	13½	15	16½	18	19½	21	22½	24	25½	27	28	29
60	3	4½	6	7½	9	10½	12	13½	15	16½	18	19½	21	22½	24	25½	27	28½	29½
61	3	4½	6	7½	9	10½	12	13½	15	16½	18	19½	21	22½	24	25½	27	28½	30
62	3	4½	6	7½	9	10½	12	13½	15	16½	18	19½	21	22½	24	25½	27	28½	30
63	3	4½	6	7½	9	10½	12	13½	15	16½	18	19½	21	22½	24	25½	27	28½	30
64	3	4½	6	7½	9	10½	12	13½	15	16½	18	19½	21	22½	24	25½	27	28½	30

Index

Also available . . .

CAREER TURNAROUND

How to apply corporate strategy techniques to your own career

John Viney & Stephanie Jones

Have you been made redundant and feel unsure about the future? Is your industry going through a tough time? Have outside influences forced you to rethink your career? Or perhaps you are secure in your job but need a new challenge? Here is *the* book for anyone who wants to revitalize their career, start taking positive action, and try something entirely new.

In this highly original approach to self-improvement, leading headhunter John Viney, and international business writer and lecturer Stephanie Jones, take these key elements of successful corporate strategies and explain how effectively they may be used to transform individual lives and careers:

- Mission Statement
- Objectives and Goals
- Personal, Company and Market Audits
- Market Research and Networking
- Product Development and Branding
- Attracting Investment
- Implementing Change

This astute strategic advice is illustrated with case studies of people from different countries and different industries who have successfully turned their careers around, proving that this approach and techniques can and *do* work.

Career Turnaround is a practical and inspiring guide to achieving positive and effective change in your career.

0 7225 2478 1   £6.99